Advance Praise

"*The Unspoken Code* provides a career roadmap for women to navigate potential workplace pitfalls and ably strive for their highest success. Marja Norris brings an honest perspective to the challenges and joys of leading a rich and full life that stays true to your core values. From finding a mentor to communicating with confidence and dressing the part, Marja imparts actionable advice on building a distinguished career for women everywhere."

–Teresa Taylor, CEO of Blue Valley Advisors LLC, author of
The Balance Myth: Rethinking Work-Life Success

"In her book, Marja drives home two particularly compelling insights: First, we are who we are as a result of all of our life experiences, including the good, the painful, and even the ugly times. And second, when we are able to tap into the precious and powerful gifts of self-discovery, honest self-study, and self-acceptance, we become poised to carve out a life of authenticity, meaning, and purpose; of making a difference in others' lives; and of lasting success, both personally and as leaders."

–Paula Kliger, PhD, ABPP, President of PsychAssets

"Marja offers sound, practical, strategic advice for women focused on advancing their careers. Her tips for creating a positive professional image and building successful relationships are spot on."

–Melissa Greenwell, EVP and COO of Finish Line, Inc.,
author of *Money on the Table*

"The rules mother never taught you are now available in Marja Norris' step-by-step guide to success for professional women. This easy to read book covers the challenges and opportunities for women to succeed, in life and in business. A must read for all women who want to get better at the game of life."

—Linda Orlans, Founder and Executive Chair, Orlans Group

The
UNSPOKEN
Code

A Businesswoman's No-Nonsense Guide
to Making It in the Corporate World

MARJA NORRIS

GREENLEAF
BOOK GROUP PRESS

This publication is designed to provide accurate and authoritative information in regard to the subject matter covered. It is sold with the understanding that the publisher and author are not engaged in rendering professional services. If expert assistance is required, the services of a competent professional should be sought.

Published by Greenleaf Book Group Press
Austin, Texas
www.gbgpress.com

Distributed by Greenleaf Book Group

For ordering information or special discounts for bulk purchases, please contact Greenleaf Book Group at PO Box 91869, Austin, TX 78709, 512.891.6100.

Design and composition by Greenleaf Book Group and Kim Lance
Cover design by Greenleaf Book Group and Kim Lance
Cover image courtesy of ©Thinkstock/Hemera Collection

Cataloging-in-Publication data is available.

Print ISBN: 978-1-62634-424-2

eBook ISBN: 978-1-62634-425-9

Part of the Tree Neutral® program, which offsets the number of trees consumed in the production and printing of this book by taking proactive steps, such as planting trees in direct proportion to the number of trees used: www.treeneutral.com

Printed in the United States of America on acid-free paper

17 18 19 20 21 22   10 9 8 7 6 5 4 3 2 1

First Edition

.....

"When sleeping women wake, mountains move"

—CHINESE PROVERB

contents

introduction

.....

"You need to figure it out." My mother's quiet but firm words rang in my ears as I tried to act nonchalant at the cool age of fourteen. We were sitting in our Detroit driveway in the blue Kingswood station wagon with the engine off. The new moon on that warm summer's eve offered us little light. Figure it out? All of a sudden, it didn't feel so cool to be a teen. My mother was leaving my dad and us. Their marriage wasn't a close one. She'd fallen in love with another man, and children weren't part of the package.

My father was heartbroken, and he withdrew. There was no talk of what was happening to the kids. I was the youngest of five, and my two older sisters were out of the house. It was just my brothers and me, and we didn't talk about what was happening either. Outside of the gossip about the house on Rosemont

Street, where the mammoth elm trees lined the well-manicured professional homes like green lush tunnels, it was eerily quiet. We walked on eggshells, pretending everything was okay. There was no more intimacy between any of us. We seldom exchanged more than a casual hello. I was on my own, and it was either sink or swim. I chose to swim, but little did I know it would be like swimming upstream in a river of bubble gum.

At sixteen, I found my escape when I married a boy from the other side of the tracks. He was in the army and didn't want to go to Korea alone. Check. I packed my suitcases and moved across the world, close to the demilitarized zone in South Korea. Unauthorized spouses were not allowed to live on base, so I lived separately from my husband, in a hooch—a cement building with separate living spaces but a common outhouse. There was no running water or electric heat—only a propane camping stove. I was the only American in my hooch, which was close to the DMZ, and I learned enough Korean in the first few weeks I was there to get by. What an adventure it was. There were nights I would lie in bed with the sound of sirens rattling the glass doors, hoping they were no more than drills. The noise drowned out the sounds of the rats skittering across the rafters above.

After a two-year stint, I was happy to leave there. I left the marriage another year later due to abuse. But there was another reason to change my path—I had given birth to the light of my life, my son Larry.

To Sink or Swim

When I returned to Detroit at eighteen years old, I knew I was behind the eight ball. My parents had sold the home I grew up in while I was away. Everything I once had was gone; I'd have to start all over. My childhood friends were all away at college. I had my one-year-old child in tow and no university education, no job, and no financial support. I knew I didn't have any skills yet, but my experience in Korea taught me an important lesson: You have to make do with the tools you have and run with them. Failing was not an option.

During my childhood, my father ran a funeral home, and the way he operated his business left an impact on me. I watched as he treated his grieving customers with the utmost respect and care. To be successful in this business, your interpersonal skills have to be one of your greatest strengths. I also learned the value of hard work. The funeral business is 24-7, and we all chipped in to make the business a success, whether that meant weeding the sanctuary lawn, answering calls, or writing out the bills while my father signed the checks. Although growing up in this environment may have caused me to miss out on typical childhood memories, it also taught me how to survive and be strong.

I wanted nothing more than to give my son a good life. I wanted us not only to survive but to thrive. I knew it would be critical to find a field offering advancement. While the funeral home paid the bills, my father's true passion was the stock market. He had a seat on the MidAmerica Commodity

Exchange and traded there as more than just a hobby. This passion seemed to be genetic: Uncle Leo said if we gave him a hundred dollars, he'd guarantee he wouldn't lose it. Aunt Ella lived next to the funeral home, and we'd often go over to her house while funerals were going on. I can still picture her reading her *Wall Street Journal* with her magnifying glass to check her stock prices and arguing with her broker to negotiate a better price. All of this made for exciting conversation around the kitchen table, and these memories came to mind upon my return from Korea. So, taking a cue from my family, at the young age of nineteen, I decided I'd make it my goal to build a career for myself in the field of finance.

One year after returning to Detroit, I began taking college night classes while working as a restaurant server and then as a proofreader. I was barely making ends meet, but we were surviving. After a few months, an opportunity opened up. My father was at his stockbroker's office, E. F. Hutton, and was told they were looking for assistants. Knowing how driven I was, he suggested I apply. I got the job—and the pay cut that came with it. But I trusted that this would be my first real step toward a vital career opportunity.

I was nervous and excited to enter this new phase of my professional life and was prepared to face what I thought would be my biggest hurdle—overcoming my fledgling skills—head on. However, I soon realized that an even greater hurdle awaited me: the simple fact of my being a woman in a workplace dominated by the opposite sex.

The moment I walked into that office for the first time is forever etched into my memory: I saw ninety-five stockbrokers, all men, walking around with a smooth confidence that completely eluded me. Men occupied every single one of the outside offices while the females took the cubicles in the middle, along with the younger male trainees. The expectation was clear and excruciatingly visible: The women were there to support the men, not the other way around. I even noticed the separation on the one-sheet listing of phone numbers. The top half listed the advisors—all men. The bottom half listed assistants—all women. It all felt like a high school dance: boys on one side, girls on the other. And the boys had all the power.

While it was hard not to feel intimidated, I didn't let it discourage me. I had seen my position as an assistant as a stepping-stone on the way to something greater, and I refused to let these feelings get the best of me. Two years into the job, I approached my manager about becoming a stockbroker. Most brokers in training entered the firm's training program and were paid to study and attend classes. My manager didn't offer me this opportunity; instead, he handed me the training manuals and said, "You can study on your own time, if you have an interest."

The training manuals were thick and overwhelming. I studied on my lunch hours in the conference room and every night after tucking my little guy into bed. One particular day, I went into the conference room on my lunch hour to study. At the other end of the room were two male employees from the training program, recognizable from their stack of books. They chatted for the hour about anything but their studies, and one of the men was doodling on his book, coloring the illustrations with his pen. *Seriously?* These men were being paid a salary to study and had time to chitchat and doodle, while I was squeezing my studies into a full-time workload and struggling to make ends meet. This reality only strengthened my resolve to become successful in a male-dominated business world.

It seemed my manager hadn't taken my commitment to studying for the exam seriously, because once I took the test and passed, they didn't know what to do with me. There were no congratulations or company announcements as there had been for my male counterparts, but I was ecstatic and ready to start my career as a financial advisor. So, I approached the advisors I'd been working for and asked for a meeting. When I shared my desire to become a full-time advisor, they laughed and told me they wanted to keep me as their assistant. We settled on a hybrid sort of arrangement: I would remain working for the two advisors but as a registered Series 7 assistant for three more years.

After that period of time, I felt I had earned a better arrangement. Word got out. I was asked by another advisor in the company to join his team as a full-time junior partner, and I accepted. No counteroffer needed to be made. A year later, when E. F. Hutton was bought out by Shearson

Lehman Brothers, many of its employees left for a company called PaineWebber, including me. While at PaineWebber, I eventually obtained a two-year Certified Financial Planning certification and later another two-year Certified Investment Manager Analyst certification, a challenging accomplishment for even those with a master's degree in business administration (MBA). After years of proving my skills over and over, I had finally reached the major leagues in the professional world.

Numbers Aren't Everything

Fast-forward thirty years: There are more women in my office than I saw in the entire first decade of my career. Women are serious about their professions and thirst to be at the top in their fields. Women's labor force participation increased by 53 percent from 1968 to 2012, and from 1980 to 2014, the number of dual-income households rose by 51 percent.[1] Not only is the number of women in the workforce increasing, but it's also been proven time and time again that gender-diverse teams get the best results. A study on European firms showed almost 20 percent higher stock prices over two years' time for companies with a greater diversity of business leaders.[2]

---

1   "Women in the Labor Force: A Databook," US Bureau of Labor Statistics, December 2015, Report 1059.

2   Mary Curtis, Christine Schmid, and Marion Struber, "Gender Diversity and Corporate Performance," Zurich, Switzerland: Credit Suisse AG Research Institute, 2009, PDF.

More women in the workplace bring a valuable parity to the bottom line.

Based on these facts, women have a lot to celebrate. We've come a long way, baby! . . . Or have we?

Dig a little bit deeper and the reality becomes clear: We still have a long way to go before we reach true equality in the workplace. Despite these encouraging numbers, women have barely moved the needle when it comes to upper management positions, political offices, and appointments on boards of directors. Women make up 59 percent of the college-educated, entry-level workforce. However, in 1980 there were *no* women in the top executive ranks of the Fortune 100 companies, and by 2001, a mere 11 percent of those corporate leaders were women. In 2016, only 15 percent of executive officers were women, and women held only 17 percent of Fortune 500 board seats.

In the financial services industry, for example, though women comprise 54 percent of the labor force, most are assistants. Only 12 percent are executive officers, and 18 percent serve on boards of directors. Interestingly enough, a catalyst study found that publicly traded companies with three or more women directors outperformed those with no women directors (as measured by the return of equity, sales, or invested capital). The more diverse the management teams are, the more they deliver higher returns for shareholders across industries.[3] In 2014, *none* were CEOs.

Although our world has progressed in the last few decades, women still earn less than men and have less power in the workplace. What's impeding our progress?

Across the board, women express frustration for not feeling validated, not being included in the decision-making process, and not being heard in meetings. Their frustration is justified: The business world was built by and for men, and men continue to dominate and dictate workplace culture. In her book *Play Like a Man, Win Like a Woman*, Gail Evans writes, "It wasn't that [men] deliberately ignored women, or disliked what women had to say. Rather, as business culture developed, few women were around to help. Men wrote all the rules because they wrote them alone." And these rules continue to be perpetuated. Many MBA programs are still based on teachings from the 1980s—a time when women were a minority in the business world.

We may be able to learn this rule book in business school or on the job—we may even be able to master it, and many have. But based on the numbers alone, women are still clearly missing a piece of the puzzle. We are competing in a workforce where key rules and practices remain in the hands of our male counterparts—obscure, unclear, and unwritten. Universities

---

3 Judith Warner, "Fact Sheet: The Women's Leadership Gap," Center for American Progress, March 7, 2014, https://www.americanprogress.org/issues/women/reports/2014/03/07/85457/fact-sheet-the-womens-leadership-gap/.

aren't set up for classes to teach women these skills, so where do we go? There's an unspoken code, and we're still missing it, even after all these years.

Making the System Work for Women

Let's pause here to acknowledge the obvious: Our lives as women are so different than men's. Speaking to an audience of a thousand women advisors from across the country at the Barron's Top 100 Women Financial Advisors Conference in 2007, Sallie Krawcheck, then CEO of Smith Barney, shared a story that represents what it's like for a woman on a business trip. On this particular day, Sallie was to meet her colleagues downstairs at seven a.m. in the lobby of the hotel. She was up at 4:30, showered, styled her hair, put on her makeup, packed her suitcase, called home to make sure the kids had their lunches and homework ready, gazed down to find a run in her hose, quickly changed her hose, dashed for the elevator, and felt her clothes stick to her skin because of the sweat from rushing around. Sallie met her colleagues downstairs at 6:59 a.m. When she asked what time they got up, none of them had gotten up before 6:30 a.m. The female audience roared with laughter; as professional women, we could all relate.

It feels as if the odds are stacked against us due to the varied demands on our time as caregivers, which means we have to work harder and longer than our male counterparts. More often than not, we are the ones who make sure the children are fed, clothed, and taken care of. We take them to the doctors, and we take off work when they're sick. We manage the family's calendar. We're usually the ones that make sure the dog gets walked and arrange for the animals to go to the vet. We attend the teacher conferences, perform the charity work, look in on our parents, send cards, buy gifts, and manage the household. And, of course, we can't forget rushing to sign up before the other working moms for beverages or paper products to bring to kids' school events, instead of being left with homemade cupcakes. We just have *more to do*. For the most part, we wouldn't have it any other way. But the extra demands on our time mean our perspective is different than that of men when it comes to work.

My most successful friends and I get together now and then for dinner to talk about women's issues at work. Our goal is to bring to light what goes unspoken—to talk about the things we see and experience but don't say out loud. What mistakes do we see happening today? How do we strike a balance? What tough choices do we make? What was the best advice we received? We all share the typical stories, such as not being taken seriously in meetings by our male colleagues and having too much on our plates. These are the obvious issues. But something else we know, despite our vastly different experiences and backgrounds in the professional world, is that when women don't have a sense of the unwritten rules of business, they limit their potential for advancement and often doom themselves to a short and undistinguished career. If we knew them, these rules would affect everything about how we present ourselves to the world, from our attitude to our communication style to the way we dress.

As my peer Harriet Shakir, an IBM executive, life coach, and the 2015 Woman of Color in Science, Technology, Engineering, and Math award winner noted, "If a woman offers to go out to pick up lunch for a meeting, she doesn't give the impression she's serious about time management. As we aim for equality, we have to carry ourselves as equals."

Alicia Masse of Alderney Advisors, senior financial analyst in analytics, chimed in: "Men come to work dressed in suits and ties, and more recently, in business casual attire. This is how men present themselves, with very little deviation. A woman has many more choices; she must be careful and exercise good judgment. If a woman dresses in a short and nonbusinesslike swingy skirt and wedge shoes, she can greatly diminish her creditability in a business setting."

Navigating the male-dominated world of business can be a labyrinthine process, and every woman I've ever talked to who is in the business world has her share of horror stories. We plowed through and learned from our mistakes. With every year, we understood the unspoken code better and better. But I can't help but wonder where we'd be if we would've known the rules sooner.

Yes: Our lives as businesswomen are different than men's.

And yes: In an ideal world, business culture would shift dramatically to allow for a diversity of paths leading to the top. But this book isn't about an ideal world: It's about working within the constraints of the world we have now. Women shouldn't have to fit in to any one standard of professionalism, particularly one that has been defined for them by their male counterparts. But consider this: Successful men are not incented to change or fix a system that's served them well. Why would they? Asking them to change is like walking into a Super Bowl locker room and proposing that the rules need to be different. "What are you doing in here?" the players would stammer. "We're already successful." The sooner we acknowledge this reality, the quicker we will find ways to work within it.

The Unspoken Code

What goes unspoken is this: There are underlying male-oriented rules and expectations in the workplace that nobody is going to tell you about. But if you aren't aware of them, you'll likely never make it to the top of the ladder. Yes, it's unfair. And that's why nobody's talking about it. At a seminar I attended recently, Dr. Lissa Young, assistant professor of leadership and management at the United States Military Academy at West Point, explained the challenges minorities face in business. She said that minorities cannot be average in their chosen career. It's okay to be a majority and be average—but minorities have to be better. That's just the way it is. Like it or not, as a woman, you have to learn and adapt to the ins and outs of your professional environment before you can reach a level of power that will allow you to push the envelope toward something more diverse and inclusive.

I remember when I started out at PaineWebber and the office space was getting tight. Another female advisor and I were told our offices were needed to make room for some new advisors. They turned the break room into a shared office—our desks side by side. We worked there as other employees walked in and out, often in conversations on the way to the pop machine. It was laughably unfair, but I said nothing and did not complain. Instead, I worked harder than ever. Did I like sitting there? No. Were the people in the office waiting for some female drama? Yes. Did they see drama? No. Had it gone on for a year, or had they put an employee of our same level in an office, I would have felt differently and taken different action. But I was in this for the long haul, and this strategy helped me be seen as a team player and gain respect from the men in the office. Noted. Check.

A culture shift won't happen over months or years—and maybe even decades—unless we do something differently today. Instead of waiting for the culture to open up to accommodate for the female perspective, I propose we learn the unspoken code of business and make it work for us. This code is about understanding the behaviors that differentiate power players from the rest of the pack. It's about exuding

confidence from the inside out. It's about building assertiveness and flexing communication skills and conveying a professional image. Because the business world was built by men,
for men, they begin their careers from a position of compara-
tive advantage and understand much of these behaviors intuitively. They've been socialized for it. The workplace expects
this behavior from its leaders, and while that may change
in the future, I believe we must work to meet the expectations *right now*. The aim of this book is to empower you to
do just that. It will guide you to strengthen your muscles and
enable you to leap over the hurdles of any misconceptions
that women can't be leaders or can't go after and obtain their
dreams. You don't know what you don't know—let's abolish
that here and now. You *will* know.

Thousands of books have been written over the years on
confidence, communication, dressing for success, and dealing with the sometimes-brutal business world, but too many
important rules concerning our careers remain unarticulated.
These rules can be uncomfortable to talk about and, not to
mention, controversial. But I believe that without being direct
and realistic about expectations, the male-dominated business
world will persist.

Women's views and approaches make this world a better,
kinder, more rewarding place to live and work. The shift is happening, but it's not happening fast enough. So let's make our
voices heard by eliminating the elements of our professional
lives that prevent others from hearing. Let's acknowledge

stereotypes then subvert them by being mindful and aware of how we unconsciously feed into them in our daily routines. Let's learn how to convey our self-confidence in a way that it won't be mistaken for anything else.

What You'll Find in This Book

Whether you are just starting out or you've been in the business world for a while and feel stuck, this book contains the best advice you can quickly seek to achieve the success you want. Each of this book's three sections will help you build a confident self-image from the inside out, from your attitude to your appearance, while continuing to acknowledge your unique status as a woman in business. Each chapter provides specific actions to take, checklists to modify to fit you, and ways to create change and enlarge your life. You'll find tips for time management and tools that transcend the workplace that will help you in all areas of your life. Use this text as a guidebook that you can come back to over and over again, as needed.

Women are more scrutinized than men, and people notice because there aren't as many of us in positions of power. We operate differently. While 80 percent of men will ask for a promotion, only 60 percent of women will.[4] No doubt there are numerous societal reasons for this, but if we don't behave like a top executive, we're not going to reach the top. Women must drop the negative self-sabotaging behaviors that work against us. We must sit at the table as equals, regardless of who's sitting there with us. We must own and be proud of the unique attributes we offer our firms and our clients as women. We need to own our strengths but be aware of what we can do differently or better to be successful.

You are your walking business card and the CEO of your career. You create your image, which becomes your brand, which can make or break your success. Embrace the three-part strategy found in this book and take charge of the unspoken code of business. Enhance your vision of who you are. You'll find the long-term personal and professional success you seek and deserve. It's time for your breakthrough—so let's get down to business.

---

4   William Jordan, "Time to Lean In? Women Lag behind Men in Seeking Advancement at Work," YouGov, November 3, 2013, https://yougov.co.uk/news/2013/11/03/time-lean-women-behind-men-seeking-advancement-wor/.

PART ONE

Setting Yourself Up for Success

Chapter One

the ABCs of awakening your own power

.....

"We cannot change what we are not aware of, and once we are aware, we cannot help but change."

−SHERYL SANDBERG, COO FACEBOOK

Take a moment to think about a few professional women you consider the most successful in their fields. Close your eyes and imagine them. What do you see? Perhaps what comes to mind first is that they always look put together, from head to toe. They're able to express their professionalism in what they wear and how they wear it. They communicate a message without saying a word. What do you hear? If you're imagining a woman at the top of her field, you probably hear a voice that's clear, articulate, and personable. Somehow, these women manage to find the right thing to say in any situation, whether they're in a boardroom argument or speaking in a casual conversation at a holiday party. Style and communication are hugely important and immediately recognizable aspects of a woman's professional image.

But there's something else at play in these successful females that goes unspoken and is harder to pinpoint than a nice suit jacket. This "something" breathes life into these other characteristics and markers of success and makes them all the more noticeable. This "something" informs every interaction successful females have. It's what makes them truly stand out above the rest.

This "something" is the core of success: those core personality traits that every successful businesswoman has. Success begins with them and radiates from them. In this first chapter, you'll begin to learn the Unspoken Code of success, starting from the inside out. These are the ABCs of your future: attitude, behavior, and confidence. Harness these traits, and you will have a successful foundation to build upon.

A Is for Attitude

.....

"There is little difference in people, but that little difference makes a big difference. The little difference is attitude. The big difference is whether it is positive or negative."

—W. CLEMENT STONE, AUTHOR, BUSINESSMAN,

AND PHILANTHROPIST

When it comes to interpersonal relationships, we often find ourselves navigating through a triangle of negativity where we act out either as a bully, victim, or rescuer.[5] If we are not conscious of our attitudes, these roles begin to inform every element of our lives, both personally and professionally. When we step out of the triangle, we stop reacting and start acting. We stop allowing our buttons to be pushed and instead set the stage for a healthier space of communication and engagement. Therefore, the first step to awakening our own power is to shift our attitude toward action and away from reaction.

As an example, my husband and I recently made plans to meet for dinner after work. Before leaving for the office that morning, I put my coffee cup in the kitchen sink while I finished getting ready for the day. As I walked out the door a little later, my husband tartly said, "Why'd you leave your coffee cup in the sink?" I thought, *Seriously? It's a freaking coffee cup.* My instinct was to let myself be angry with him all day. I sulked for a bit, but then I realized I was caught up in my own victim story. *Okay. What am I going to do . . . double dip by ruining my day? I think not.* So I let it go by changing my attitude, and my day was a productive and happy one. I was able to mentally step outside of the "victim triangle" and see the circumstance for what it really was.

Later that evening, however, as I was getting ready to meet my husband for dinner, those negative feelings rushed back. I

---

5   Robert Taibbi, "The Relationship Triangle," *Psychology Today*, June 21, 2011, https://www.psychologytoday.com/blog/fixing-families/201106/the-relationship-triangle.

thought, *Geez, I don't even want to eat with this man after he gave me such a hard time about a coffee cup when I clearly have a million other things on my mind.* I knew that if I let them, these thoughts would cast a negative light on the rest of the evening. That was my choice to make: I could let my own negative emotions get the better of me and react accordingly, or I could find a way to handle my frustrations in a more productive and mindful way, thus acting from a place of strength. So I asked myself: *What will happen if I change my attitude, here and now?* This awareness provides an opportunity to check in with what's really going on and make a decision based on facts rather than unchecked emotions.

Over dinner, I brought up our earlier exchange, asking him, "What was really bothering you this morning?" Jerry told me it had nothing to do with me. He admittedly had something else on his mind and took it out on me. Because I let go of anger and rationally raised the issue, he could acknowledge what he was feeling. He then apologized. What had started out as a problem turned out to be an opportunity for us to connect. Instead of holding on to that anger for longer and taking it personally, I shifted my attitude and we had an engaging night together.

THE ATTITUDE SHIFT

What is your attitude? Is it generally positive or is some self-examination in order? Consciously or unconsciously maintaining a negative attitude creates unnecessary chaos and stress. You've got enough stress in your life with all that you're juggling. Shifting your attitude toward the positive will make life easier in countless ways.

.....

> *"Your attitude, not your aptitude, will determine your altitude."*
>
> −ZIG ZIGLAR

Webster's dictionary defines attitude as "a mental position, feeling, or emotion regarding a fact or a state." Put another way, attitude is how we choose to perceive the infinite number of inputs and events that surround us at any given moment. Usually, these inputs are neither bad nor good, negative nor positive—they're arbitrary until we place them in the larger context of our day, week, or month and begin to infuse them with meaning.

Let's use a red light as an example. On its own, the stop-light turning from green to red is a simple directive that moves traffic along. But if you're running late and rushing to get to work, each red light you encounter suddenly turns into a serious hindrance. It becomes an object of our anger, and we react accordingly.

Unfortunately, once we react to one input or event, it becomes all too easy to infuse all others that follow with that same negativity. It's no longer simply that you're late or that the stoplight held you up. Every minor detail suddenly becomes a hindrance to functioning at your best: the sticky elevator key, the too-talkative coworker, the boss's loud voice, your husband's coffee cup commentary . . . the list, as we've all experienced, goes on and on. Once you're stuck in a cloud of negativity, it can feel impossible to exit. It permeates everything and everyone around you. Allowing yourself to exist in this negative cloud changes how you view situations, people, and important decisions you need to make. This is not a good thing. In fact, it can have downright detrimental consequences.

HARD TRUTHS

In any male-dominated profession, the male's perspective is the default. It's not fair, but it's the truth. And although they may try not to, men often bring their stereotypical underlying views of women into the workplace. Well, we don't have time to wait for them to change. Instead, we need to do what we can right now to show them that these stereotypes are wrong. Yes, this is a double standard. Every professional should work to be polite and positive, not rude or moody, and every professional should be given some slack when they falter. When men get angry, they're "passionate" or they're standing up for themselves. When women get angry, we're "too emotional," or worse, we're "bitchy." When women slip up, it reinforces what men assume about women already: This is confirmation bias. We need to stop ourselves from giving men the chance to make these wrong assumptions. Because of this bias against women, we need to be cognizant of our higher level of emotions and choose to uplift ourselves. Use humor like a Superwoman attitude of not letting circumstances get to you and an awareness of your control to climb out and up. Check.

When my husband commented on my placement of the coffee mug in the sink, I was able to choose how I'd react, instead of simply reacting. The mindfulness required to choose positivity over negativity is a habit that takes years to cultivate. When I first started out in the business world, this was not an easy task, but I knew that in order to get to where I wanted I had no other choice. That's how crucial attitude is to success.

CHOOSING A POSITIVE ATTITUDE

When I first started my career as a businesswoman, I was raising a son alone, totally broke, and driving a long daily commute. I didn't feel I had much going for me. I often looked around at the successful executives as I swiftly walked from the parking garage to the banks of elevators and felt my life couldn't be more different than theirs. I was nineteen and coming out of an abusive marriage. I was a divorced, single mom receiving no child support, with no help from either family in watching my son, and working two jobs to pay my bills. I forced myself to smile. One day, an advisor in my office, Norm, asked me, "With everything going on, how do you stay so positive?" I looked at him and mustered, "Staying positive is a choice."

As a woman in a male-dominated field, I knew I faced

more challenges than my male counterparts. I had to give it everything I had, which wasn't a lot. Outside of honesty and a willingness to learn and work hard, I had a positive attitude that I worked hard to perfect. Of course I had negative feelings about my situation, but I refused to let them define my life. I knew if I didn't maintain my positive attitude, I might fall apart. So to some degree, I faked it. If you can pull out a positive attitude in the midst of chaos, people will wonder what you've been up to and want some too.

We've been told bottling up feelings can lead to health issues such as muscle tension, high blood pressure, hormone imbalances, insomnia, and low self-esteem—none of which any of us can afford to entertain for long. Denying feelings is unhealthy—but we can't allow them to cripple us, ruining our lives and relationships. But maintaining a positive attitude does not require you to neglect your emotions. It simply requires a more mindful approach to the way we react toward those countless inputs. It requires us to make that mental shift—to step back when we feel ourselves becoming frustrated and ask ourselves, *Is this the most productive way to manage this emotion right now? Can this wait?*

An emotional hangover is evidence of a bad attitude. Once your mind clears, you feel guilty for losing your cool, whether publicly or privately. Deferring your frustrations until you're in a safer place to express them can be a liberating experience—and one you won't feel guilty about. One particularly frustrating day when I was driving home from work feeling overwhelmed, I allowed myself a good, long cry. Afterward, I felt better and was able to move on.

No fairy godmother will make your dreams of success come true. That's something you must do for yourself, and it's something you must strive for. In this way, maintaining a positive attitude is about mindfulness—but it's also about holding yourself accountable. You can't always choose your circumstances, but you *can* choose how you react to those circumstances. Attitude is one of the few aspects of life over which you have total control. And controlling it will work in your favor in countless ways, both personally and professionally. Don't lose out on opportunity by succumbing to feelings that the whole world—from the stoplight to the overpressured boss—is out to get you. Take accountability for your mindset, and be aware of the triangle of negative attitudes. If you choose to take control, your life will change for the better. Step back for a moment. Breathe. Shift and refocus. Smile. *If at first your smile isn't genuine, that's okay.* Smile anyway. The next time something or someone upsets you, take a few deep breaths and intentionally shift the feeling from negative to positive.

Have you ever talked to a frazzled businesswoman? (Remember our full plates.) Men tend to want to get out of her way. They don't talk about this issue of avoidance, but no doubt it's there. Shifting your attitude to a positive one and keeping it there helps to remove this stigma that women are more emotional.

.....

> *"If you put your problems in a paper bag with all the*
> *rest of the world's problems and shake the bag up*
> *to see what your new problems will be, you'll likely*
> *decide to quickly take your own problems back."*
>
> –BONNIE ROLLINS

If you're stressed about the stock market trending down, for example, turn your thoughts toward what a privilege it is to have money to invest. If you feel anger or sadness, recall a time when you've felt peace or happiness. Allow yourself to feel the emotion, but then let it go. If you need to, return to it at a time when you can process it more fully. Acting as a victim by letting whoever upset you take up space in your head gives *away* your power. Focus on what you *do* have and on the things for which you are grateful. Make the shift. Tough days are what give good days their radiance.

VISUALIZATION EXERCISES FOR A WINNING ATTITUDE

My friend and business coach, and someone who is partly responsible for the success of my marriage and business partnership solvency, is Larry Miller of Momentum Coaching. Following are two visualization techniques Larry taught me to get through tough times:

Visualization 1: Joyful, Easy, Successful, Sustained, Integrated, and Important

Feelings and emotions are the most powerful communication mediums within our conscious and subconscious minds. Imagination and visualization can allow you to physically experience—in your body, mind, and spirit—how success feels. Start by visualizing, imagining the outcome you want in a given situation. Next, verbalize this visualization. For example, say to yourself, "I am handling this meeting with ease, and my boss congratulates me on the job well done." Say it out loud. Then, let it play in your mind like a movie to form a mental picture, so you actually see and feel your success. Do it a few times, until you're confident that you succeed. You have to *feel* it, not only picture it or think it or verbalize it. How does it physically and emotionally feel to accomplish your goal? If it doesn't feel natural at first, play it over in your head until it does. End the visual exercise with a feeling of gratitude; this is the most important of all.

Positive affirmations work when you eliminate the words *try* and *want* from your vocabulary. These words lack commitment and feeling. It's not enough to say, "I'm going to *try* to get through this" or, "I *want* to stop being angry about that." How does trying *feel*? How does wanting *feel*? What you feel is what you'll get. You can get stuck in trying or wanting, or you can decide to *feel* successful. It's your choice.

Here are the steps for the JESSII (Joyful, Easy, Successful, Sustained, Integrated, and Important) visualization and feeling exercise. This exercise takes no more than five minutes—you can do it while you're driving, waiting for an appointment, getting ready in the morning, or anytime.

Continued

- **Step 1:** Envision the outcome you prefer, knowing how joyful, easy, successful, sustained, integrated, and important it is (JESSII).
- **Step 2:** Speak the outcome out loud, using the present tense and a positive tone.
- **Step 3:** Play the scene through; see and feel yourself succeeding.
- **Step 4:** Repeat the scene until you're confident that you are successful.
- **Step 5:** Feel and express appreciation for what this is bringing to your life.

Keep index cards with these steps written out in brief. Anytime you feel down, go through the exercise by acknowledging what is causing the bad attitude. With a sense of gratitude, refocus your mind and feelings on what you prefer the outcome to be, not only for today, but throughout your life. Take charge of your emotions and feel clear, confident, and certain. When you are ready to visualize, post these steps where you can see them, such as in your car, at your desk, or somewhere on your phone.

Visualization 2: Respect the Wall—It's There to Guide You

Larry explains an important analogy: "Do race car drivers know that there's a cement wall next to them while they're driving two hundred miles an hour? Of course they do. It's there to warn them, not to crash into. Rather than fear the wall, they respect the wall, even value the wall for guidance."

The same philosophy applies when you're under pressure and feeling emotional. Like the cement wall, your emotions should guide you, not run your life. They can be your best friend, instead of your enemy. They tell you what you need to know, not what you feel like hearing. Emotions are a wake-up call, telling you that there's something you need to address, not a weight to carry around your neck. How we respond to our emotions—whether we fear them or respect their feedback and guidance—is the difference between victimhood and self-empowerment.

As Larry puts it, "Feeling an uncomfortable emotion like fear or anxiety is a feedback signal that something is out of alignment with our core values and intentions. The emotion is checking to be sure that you have everything under control. Imagine you're driving your car down the freeway and drift off to the right on the bumpy strips on the side of the road. The bumpy strips have a noisy, bouncy response to the car wheels. It is their job to be irritating, to grab our attention and let us know we are off course a bit. And we choose our response to them. We can be irritated at the noise and bouncing of our car, even voice a few profanities in response. Or we can choose to be grateful for their feedback, jarring as it might be. We can choose to feel relief and gratitude for their interruption—they're just doing their job to keep us alert and on course when we seem to have wandered a bit. Feeling the emotions and then letting them know you are back on track and have it handled will let them relax and go quietly back on sentry duty. Ignoring them will only invite them to continue their interruption and respond even more forcefully until they feel heard. While some days you may have enough uncomfortable thoughts and feelings to fill a bus, you're always the one driving. Don't ignore the turbulence

Continued

that enters your mind and affects your feelings, because the longer you ignore it, the bigger it becomes. Welcome it, appreciate this message you've been given, and then remember that you are the driver of the car, no matter how many concerned passengers you have."

.....

"Every thought we think is creating our future."

–LOUISE L. HAY

No matter what your circumstances, your attitude is a choice you make that affects everything you do. The way you choose to respond to feelings of frustration, pity, anger, or aggravation will affect your day, life, and health. Unfortunately, the way you respond can also feed into the exact stereotypes we as women are trying to subvert every day. Men should do their part to stop making wrong assumptions about women, but in the meantime, we need to acknowledge the Unspoken Code that every time we have a bad attitude we're displaying the very actions that some men have come to expect. Let's put a stop to this by being mindful and shifting our attitude toward something more positive.

B Is for Behavior

.....

"Behavior is a mirror in which everyone
displays his [her] own image."

−JOHANN WOLFGANG VON GOETHE

Attitude involves our chosen mental state, experience, teachings, or environment. Behavior is the action or inaction we take that is influenced by our attitude. Controlling our behavior is a central component in workplace and personal success. Your behavior in the workplace is judged by whether you're meeting, not meeting, or exceeding the company's goals set forth for your position in performance reviews. Whoever you report to, whether it's your superior, a board, or company stockholders, will reward positive behavior. As you exceed expectations through disciplined behavior, the likelihood for advancement is high. Positive behavior results in personal success, whether it's in relationships, taking care of your health, or finances. True success isn't measured by wealth, a prestigious position, a happy relationship, or family. True success is the balance of success in all areas of your life, and that loops back to how behavior most often follows attitude.

Behavior is what you say and what you do. It's how you conduct yourself, your mannerisms, how you respond to what is going on around you, and how you interact with others. Behavior can convey emotional intelligence and show that you are a professional—that you are curious, polite, and open, especially when faced with a challenging situation.

Psychologist Nicholas Humphrey believes that social intelligence, rather than quantitative intelligence, truly defines human beings.[6] Human behavior relies on an individual's intelligence quotient (IQ), emotional quotient (EQ), and social quotient (SQ). Everyone knows IQ and EQ are important when problem solving and dealing with other people, but the SQ is equally important, because it demonstrates your level of capability when functioning in complex social situations. For example, you can have a high IQ and even a relatively high EQ, but if you can't gracefully socialize with fellow executives, clients, or potential clients, you're going to fall flat on your face. If you're trying to get a budget approval to fund your brilliant project, an aloof personality or lack of social graces can be critically damaging to your goals and career.

How we behave is a large part of what puts us in or out of the advancement pool. Unprofessional behaviors like gossiping, talking excessively about your personal life, addiction to technology, giving excuses for laziness, acting like a prima donna, flirting, instigating rebellion, or complaining not only send the wrong message, they can also cost you your career. On the other hand, behaviors that make a positive professional impression—having a positive attitude, being detailed,

---

6   Henrike Moll and Michael Tomasello, "Cooperation and Human Cognition: The Vygotskian Intelligence Hypothesis," *Philosophical Transactions of the Royal Society* 362, no. 1480 (2007): 639–648, doi: 10.1098/rstb.2006.2000.

being empathetic, encouraging others, displaying good manners, and carrying strong work ethics—can solidify your place in the advancement pool. You should give the kind of service and attention you want to receive. When you call someone, ask them if it's a good time to talk, and return phone calls on the same day. These are basics that every professional must master, but they are even more critical for women.

.....

"The truth is that we can learn to condition our minds, bodies and emotions to link pain or pleasure to whatever we choose. By changing what we link pain and pleasure to, we will instantly change our behaviors."

–TONY ROBBINS

BEHAVIOR 101

First and foremost, your behavior should come from a place of kindness. With kindness, you'll get far in your career. Being a kind person opens doors and attracts other people's kindness. When someone is challenging you, you want to act, not react, especially when those around you are acting unprofessional. This doesn't mean you don't stand up for yourself or you allow yourself to be taken advantage of. What it means is that you handle the situation with assertiveness, grace, decisiveness, and boldness, standing firmly for what you believe.

As we know from the previous section on attitude, how we respond to our emotions can be our greatest strength and also our greatest weakness. A friend, Pierre Corriveau, an auto executive with IHS Automotive, taught me the French term *tenir sa langue*, which means "hold your tongue" and encourages you to circle your tongue seven times on the roof of your mouth before speaking impulsively. This is excellent advice because it slows down your emotions and allows you to think before you speak. It's too easy to spout something off in the heat of the moment. Instead, take a minute to slow down, check your emotions, and speak with purpose. It will help ensure that you don't say something you might regret.

Because of our endless differences, such as gender, religious beliefs, upbringing, nationality, and so on, everyone speaks a different language. Be aware of who you're speaking to and be socially savvy and sensitive to others in any given situation. For example, if you know that you're meeting with someone who is always busy and likes to get to the point, keep small talk to a minimum. You're likely to have only a minute or two to make your point before you lose their attention. Because you know they want the bottom line, social intelligence in that situation means being aware of this person's communication style and complying with it.

My friend and spiritual teacher Ellen Miller heads a circle for women, Changing Woman Sisterhood. She's taught me so much about looking at our learned behaviors. One day, when I was sitting in circle with Ellen, we talked at length about men and our differences. When I mentioned how they should change to be more supportive of women, her response surprised me. Ellen said, "No, you have to change. It's up to you to shift." "What?" the feminist in me stammered. Ellen continued, "Marja, yes, in theory, that's true. But it's just not going to happen. So get over it and become responsible for yourself. You shift. When you shift, everyone else shifts." It's true. There I was, pointing one finger out with the other three pointing back at me. I realized it wasn't power over a man I wanted—I wanted power over myself. We must shift our behavior the same way we shift our attitude.

Ellen changed my paradigm on self-accountability with these simple but powerful words: *The shift starts with you.* It's said that our behaviors are a culmination of the seven generations that come before us. Our current behaviors will affect seven generations into the future. If that doesn't give you an awareness and reason to change today, what will? Ask yourself how your current behaviors have served you. Then focus on how you would like your behavior to be. This calls for self-awareness and a willingness to replace negative and self-defeating behaviors with positive and self-empowering behaviors. That shift takes a conscious effort and confident self-mastery. This is a lifelong learning process. When you screw up, learn from it and move on—that is your goal. Trust me, you'll always have another chance to practice shifting your behaviors.

When you are working to better yourself, becoming self-aware, making change, and looking for those new opportunities, it can be easy to blame others. While this may be human nature, doing so doesn't shift things for you. The only person you can change is you. However, more often than not, when you behave differently, the people around you will behave differently as well. They can't help but shift because your responses come from a better place. If you approach others with kindness, most people will respond in kind. If you are professional in your behavior and are approachable and assertive about what you have to offer, you're going to be taken seriously. You're going to get that promotion, that seat at the table, or that new client. You're going to get ahead, or you will gain the clarity you need to move to a company that will support you. No more feeling stuck.

.....

"The most common way people give up their power is thinking they don't have any."

—ALICE WALKER

GET UNCOMFORTABLE

Sometimes in business, you have to be willing to be uncomfortable—to be courageous, even nervous, and step out of your comfort zone, learning a new skill set, taking on a new position, delivering a large presentation, or obtaining a big-name client or a large company purchase. Your willingness to take on these situations displays belief in yourself, and it becomes confidence when the task at hand is successful. Women have a tendency to take less risk, and this behavior can hurt us in the workplace. Learn how to be comfortable with uncomfortable emotions and new experiences. It makes you a better person and a more valuable employee.

.....

"Fear is a sign—usually a sign that I'm doing something right."

−ERICA JONG

An acquaintance of mine who was asked to join the C-suite knows the importance of being uncomfortable. When Mary was asked to take over the position of a highly ranked executive, she was scared to death, but she did it anyway and became successful beyond her imagination.

Stepping outside your comfort zone generates positive rewards—and making yourself uncomfortable can be a powerful reminder of the connection between behavior and results. It's like giving yourself a promotion. The results allow you to set a new bar for yourself, and your confidence will grow. Once you try something new and achieve a new goal, you can't go backward. Get used to doing one uncomfortable thing a day, something simple like speaking with someone who intimidates you, reaching out to someone you feel is beyond your reach, learning a new skill, or simply eating by yourself at a nice restaurant you've been dying to try. A little discomfort is freeing; a little risk is exciting. It encourages you to constantly move toward bigger and better things.

Try these two tricks to expand your brain's capacity by simply changing your routine. Little switches like this can make you aware of the fact that you need to do things differently to reach your goals. They trigger awareness, and you can't make changes if you're not aware of what you're doing and how you can be doing it differently or better.

1. If you've been wearing your watch on your right wrist for years, try switching it to the left. Then every time you check the time, you get a little reminder that it's time for a change.

2. At work, move your mouse pad to the other side of your keyboard. You'll be reminded of the importance of being uncomfortable throughout the day. It drove my partners crazy when they popped over to my computer, but it helped me be conscious of stepping up.

.....

"One only gets to the top rung of the ladder by steadily climbing up one at a time, and suddenly all sorts of powers, all sorts of abilities which you thought never belonged to you—suddenly become within your own possibility, and you think, 'Well, I'll have a go, too.'"

—MARGARET THATCHER

POSITIVE BEHAVIOR IN YOUR FUTURE

For every action, there's an equal and opposite reaction. If you exhibit positive behavior, the action that you have control over, the energy of your action will be like a boomerang, likely coming back to you with the positive reaction you desire.

C Is for Confidence

.....

"A strong, positive self-image is the best possible preparation for success."

–CHARLES B. NEWCOMB

Have you ever noticed that professionals at the peak of their careers seem to radiate incredible charisma and confidence? They carry themselves as if they're fearless. They see the world from a different point of view. I don't need to tell you that success—getting the promotion or landing the big client—can create confidence. But successful people convey confidence even when they're just starting out, *before* they get the promotions and the benefits. It is critical that you appear to be a confident professional, even when you're just starting out. Understanding this fact is the third and final step to unlocking your inner power.

Confidence is being conscious of your power. It's about

being who you are and feeling a level of certitude in the value of your successes. Confidence in business is of the utmost importance because not only does it bolster your own performance but it also makes others feel secure about your actions. A professional's confidence level conveys their competence loud and clear.

CULTIVATING CONFIDENCE

.....

"Self-esteem isn't everything; it's just there's nothing without it."

—GLORIA STEINEM

I know from experience that confidence emanates from attitude (A) and behavior (B). I don't love public speaking. I get nervous I'll forget something, even though the audience will likely never know. I think the worst is speaking in front of your peers, bar none. Your peers know what you know, unlike sharing a topic with an audience for educational purposes, where you are the expert on your discussion. What brings self-confidence is having a positive attitude and a well-thought-out talk, practicing a lot (work behavior), and gaining experience. And you can only get experience by doing. I remember giving a talk in front of five hundred of my peers. I was on a panel with three other men. I was the most nervous, but my attitude and behavior set me up for success, even though the confidence portion wasn't quite there yet. According to the questionnaire given to the audience afterward, my portion of the talk was the best received. This gave me confidence. When I want to doubt myself, I remember this talk. In the workplace, if you are well prepared, authentic, and have a positive attitude, you'll be okay. Even among your peers.

It is said we have at least sixty thousand thoughts a day, and of those thoughts, 80 percent are negative.[7] That's pretty scary, isn't it? Most women I speak with wish they had *more confidence.* That's across the board. Negative thoughts can derail your confidence, but it's amazing how looking at the big picture and envisioning a positive outcome can make such a difference.

I used to be an expert self-sabotager. I knew what I needed to do but always shot myself in the foot by not doing the right homework or not preparing well enough, setting myself up for failure. I landed exactly where I didn't want to be. Afterward I would think, *Boy, that worked out really well. Not!* Whether it's fear of success or being too hard on yourself, this can derail your confidence. Reinstating positive self-talk during the preparation process will help you achieve a stellar outcome. Think, *If not now, when? And why not me?* Someone gets to do it; it might as well be you.

---

7   "Don't Believe Everything You Think," Cleveland Clinic Wellness (2012), accessed December 14, 2016, http://www.clevelandclinicwellness.com/programs/NewSFN/pages/default.aspx?-Lesson=3&Topic=2&UserId=00000000-0000-0000-0000-000000000705.

It may take a lot of self-talk at times, but without doing the work required to boost your confidence, you can deflate your career. Again, it starts with a shift in how you think and what you do and say. There will always be someone who is more successful, is more attractive, or has a more vital career or a more beautiful home. The list goes on and on. While you may perceive others as having more or being more than you, they may well be coveting your life—your marriage, children, health, or career. Living in a state of gratitude will build your confidence. And if your confidence wavers, know how to build it back up.

Confidence is so important to understanding the Unspoken Code that nearly every portion of this book is dedicated to building it and maintaining it. Here are some tried-and-true tips for gaining confidence:

- **Start Positive**: Start off the day with optimistic thoughts. Be aware of your mind's internal chatter. Imagine a small room full of fifty caffeinated monkeys bouncing off the walls like ping-pong balls. If you're not paying attention, negative monkey mind will go to work. Make a conscious choice to replace your negative thinking with positive thoughts. Change your inner monologue. Keep an index card with positive thoughts written on it to read. Keep the card in your bathroom or jewelry box and start each day with enthusiasm and expectations. Think of it as your BFF card, a written version of what your best friend would tell you to remind you what you're good at. Keep a second BFF card at work with three things you're proud of—compliments or positive feedback you have received from your peers, executives, or clients about your performance. Keep a copy on your phone, in your desk and purse, or wherever makes sense for you. When you need a boost, pull it out and read it to shift your brain waves from negative to positive. Think of the Winnie-the-Pooh characters. Do you want to be known as glum Eeyore or having the confidence of fun Tigger? Not that we want to have the irresponsibility of Tigger. We do not. But his unwavering self-esteem? Check.

- **Keep Positive Company**: Hang around those who make you feel good; their positive energy will rub off on you. If you hang around toxic people, the negativity will spread through you too. Be the words you want others to say to describe you when they think about you. Live by your ideals, not those of others. They can stroke your ego, but they can't build your confidence. *Only you can do that.*

- **Call It In**: Think of someone you greatly respect and call that person into your mind. How would this person handle the situation you're in? Sometimes you simply need to regroup. If you're lacking confidence, as every one of us does from time to time, taking a break may be the perfect prescription, whether it is a couple of PTO days or a ten-minute walk around the block. If you have time, check in with positive friends, family, or colleagues.

- **Make a Promise to Your Inner Child**: Find a favorite photo from when you were a little girl. Tape it somewhere you will see it every day. Mine is in a small acrylic frame with a magnet back stuck on my makeup mirror. I'm all of three years old, sitting in my hand-me-down sailor dress, holding a god-awful-looking hand-me-down doll. My eyes are squinting from the bright sun, and my smile is as big as day, in anticipation of what life has to offer. When I get knocked down, I promise her I will get up again. In my mind, I tell her how much I love her, how perfect she is just as she is, and that she is worthy. Time passes quickly, and this is no rehearsal. Your "little girl" believes in you. Deliver her dreams.

OVERCOMING IMPOSTER SYNDROME

One of the biggest hindrances to self-confidence for executive women is managing the Imposter Syndrome, which manifests as that little voice in your head saying, *Maybe they're right—I really haven't earned this, even though I think I'm qualified* or *Maybe I ought to triple check my facts because they keep telling me I don't know what I'm talking about—they must be right.* Blogger Anna Kegler acknowledges that this is a problem often specific to females.[8] Men, on the other hand, have to manage its opposite: something Kegler calls the Entitlement Syndrome. This occurs when a man overestimates his own skills relative to others and feels he deserves respect and success. If he doesn't get it, it's not his fault, unlike those with the Imposter Syndrome, who are stumbling over themselves with apologies. Sounds all too familiar, doesn't it?

As professional women, we seemingly are caught in a tug-of-war between the Imposter Syndrome and the Entitlement Syndrome. Let's dive into this by first covering the Imposter Syndrome, a term coined in 1978 by clinical psychologists Dr. Pauline R. Clance and Suzanne A. Imes. The Imposter Syndrome refers to high-achieving individuals marked by an inability to internalize their accomplishments and a persistent fear of being exposed as a fraud. Not surprising, studies show this is more common in high-achieving women versus men due to a competence bias from childhood. While boys are raised to exaggerate their skills, take risks, and fall and pick themselves back up, girls are taught to think things through and second guess, avoiding risk and failure, and to not raise their hand unless they're sure they have the right answer. And girls learn from the media that their real value is in their appearance. It's been our conditioning. Think Bernie Sanders's

8   Anna Kegler, "Hillary Clinton, Melissa Harris-Perry and the Opposite of Imposter Syndrome," *The Huffington Post* (blog), March 27, 2016, http://www.huffingtonpost.com /anna-kegler/hillary-clinton-and-the-opposite-of-imposter-syndrome_b_9553190.html.

unkempt hair with just "being Bernie" and Hillary Clinton being chastised for her pantsuits.

The opposite is the Entitlement Syndrome. The Entitlement Syndrome is formally known as the Dunning-Kruger effect, or illusory superiority. It's when a person, mostly white males, overestimates his own skills, relative to others. He believes he deserves not only respect for his accomplishments (no matter how mediocre) but also success. He doesn't have to go above and beyond to qualify for excellence, and if he doesn't get the success he deserves, it's not his fault. He doesn't internalize. Women, on the other hand, tend to attribute their success to external factors (Imposter Syndrome). When men succeed, they tend to attribute their success to inner qualities like dedication and talent (Entitlement Syndrome). When men and women fail, the attributions get flipped. Women tend to blame their failures on internal shortcomings or a lack of effort (Imposter Syndrome), while men tend to blame circumstances outside their control (Entitlement Syndrome). Mostly, men internalize their successes and women internalize their failures. This is a slippery slope for women. It takes a strong woman to be able to push through this dysfunctional cycle and not give up or play victim because she feels it's useless, with a "damned if I do and damned if I don't" mindset. Become consciously aware of your fellow women and throw them a line as often as you can. It'll be a lifeline that won't be forgotten.

In order to gain confidence, we must banish the idea that

we're not good enough or that we're frauds entirely from our minds.

One of the highest-ranking women in Congress and mother of three, Representative Cathy McMorris Rodgers, took a professional leap when she was appointed to the state legislature. Her reaction was that she wasn't ready. "I hesitated," Cathy said, "and yet other people had confidence in me. That meant a lot." Cathy came to Washington as a single thirty-five-year-old. Since then, she's built both a family (becoming the first woman to have three kids while in Congress) and a stellar career. She punched through the Imposter Syndrome many women experience.

My cousin, Tiina Perttu, CBRE program manager and recipient of numerous sales excellence awards, shares a similar tale:

"If you were to review my career path, you might notice that it's taken a few turns over the years. While I had a clear vision of becoming an interior designer in college, my work experience includes sales, color strategist, product development, clothing design, and workplace strategy. Quite a mixed bag!

"I've been fortunate to have a variety of interesting opportunities offered to me over the years—opportunities that I jumped to take. Numerous times, they were roles where I really didn't have the experience and put myself into an unknown situation.

"Often, self-doubt would plague me in these new roles. I didn't know how to own my success and would attribute it to luck. I would often worry that I wasn't fulfilling the role like my predecessor. And worst of all, I minimized the value of my work, sometimes giving it away for free.

"Even though self-doubt can still creep over me, I've learned to see the value of what I bring to the table by working with great coaches and having learned tough lessons after the fact. After 90 percent of my job opportunities over the years were due to being recruited, I finally recognized the pattern and know I must be doing something right!"

.....

"I can tell you that what you're looking for is already inside you."

–ANNE LAMOTT

People aren't born confident; they learn how to be positive and project confidence about who they are and what they are capable of. Think of a few women you consider poised and self-assured: Princess Diana, Oprah Winfrey, Jacqueline Kennedy Onassis, Rosa Parks, Condoleezza Rice, Mary Barra, Sheryl Sandberg, Amelia Earhart, Audrey Hepburn, Coco Chanel, Beyoncé Knowles, Ellen DeGeneres, and Diane Sawyer may come to mind. Whether or not they truly are confident women all the time in all circumstances is debatable, and surely each of them has suffered from Imposter Syndrome at one point or another; but what they do well is project that they are.

CREATING AN AURA OF CONFIDENCE

Having confidence creates an aura about you. Whether or not your confidence is fully authentic isn't important. Truly, no one's confidence is there 100 percent of the time. What *is* important is the aura that permeates from you. Webster's Dictionary defines *aura* as a special quality or feeling that seems to come from a person, place, or thing—a luminous radiation. As you project this aura of confidence, you project a standard not only for yourself but also for how others will treat you. It works for the executive men, so why not have it work for you, too? Next time, stand your ground when there are subliminal or underhanded messages sent your way by remembering the tale by Hans Christian Andersen, "The Emperor's New Clothes." The story is about the power of an emperor. The tale, in a nutshell, is this: Two unscrupulous weaver's claim they can weave a suit for the emperor that will appear invisible to those unfit for their jobs or are otherwise helplessly incompetent. Although none of his subjects could see the suit as they paraded it before them, nobody spoke up for fear of losing their jobs or appearing stupid. Only when a young boy cried out, "But he isn't wearing anything at all!" as the emperor paraded down the street, did anyone even think of challenging the king. So pull out that moxie of yours as businessmen have done for years. And when you're feeling less than confident, think about this tale. It's only in the eye of the beholder, like the child knew but no one else wanted to say. It'll put you in a good mental place.

Work Your ABCs

Attitude drives Behavior. When A and B are in alignment, you will be in a perfect place for C, Confidence. With the three ABCs, you can avoid many career path bumps, gain a great reputation for being someone that people want to work with, and most importantly, be empowered to accomplish anything you put your mind to. Think of these ABCs like the Venn diagram. The overlapping center is the sweet spot of the Unspoken Code of success. When you have a positive attitude, project professional behavior, and give the aura of self-confidence, the three of these combined propel you to success.

What Is No One Telling You?

THINGS TO REMEMBER:

- You are the screenwriter and movie director of your autobiography. Speak it, see it, and feel what you want your life to look like. Be in gratitude for each "take" of your film!

- A shift in your attitude shifts others toward your desired goals.

- Remember the phrase *tenir sa langue*: Think before you speak. Hold your tongue.

- Don't allow negative thoughts to sabotage what's going well.

- Keep your BFF cards handy and read those positive affirmations about yourself as often as you need.

- Don't allow anyone to dim your brightness. If they're blinded by the light of your moxie, tell them to grab their sunglasses!

- Honor your inner little girl. No one will promise, love, or believe in her more than you. Deliver those dreams.

PLAN OF ACTION

As a result of what I learned in chapter 1, I am going to

Stop doing—

- _____

- _____

Start doing—

- _____

- _____

Continue doing–

- _____

- _____

Chapter Two

the hole in your glass is leaking: your survival kit for handling it all

.....

"Most of us have trouble juggling. The woman who says she doesn't is someone whom I admire but have never met."

–BARBARA WALTERS

Your Glass Is Leaking

Multitasking is one of life's challenges that we don't have time to think about—we just do it.

I've heard it said that a career woman's life can be compared to holding a glass that has six holes in it, with each hole representing an important area of our life, for example: health, work, hobbies, spouse, kids, friends. Fill the glass with water and our five fingers won't reach all six holes. No matter what you do or how hard you try, at least one area of your life will always be leaking.

.....

"Now we know that women can do what men can do, but we don't know that men can do what women can do."

−GLORIA STEINEM, IN AN INTERVIEW WITH OPRAH WINFREY

If a woman's glass has six holes, I propose that a man's glass of water has four holes that they can cover without significant difficulty. A man can have the same career demands as a woman, but when a woman gets home, she starts her second career. As soon as she sets foot in the doorway, she transitions into the multiple roles of cook, housekeeper, shopper, and default parent, among many others. Most of us wouldn't have it any other way because of the joy we experience when we choose to live full, overflowing lives. But when we become overwhelmed by life, it can directly affect our self-esteem, which in turn affects our workplace behavior. When we are spread too thin, we are unable to give any of our priorities the attention they need. This can turn into a negative cycle that, when left unaddressed, becomes harder and harder to fix. For example, when we don't have time to exercise, our body changes, our clothes don't fit, and we regrettably may lose our self-confidence. We feel out of control—powerless over our own lives. None of us can afford this type of mindset when we're striving toward the top. While we may often struggle with imbalance, feeling frustrated and underappreciated, we can prioritize what's most important to us and organize our time accordingly.

While caregiver roles are beginning to become more egalitarian, society's general perceptions of them are not going to change to a great degree anytime soon. Businessmen continue to assume that women will find ways to juggle these roles and shoulder these extra responsibilities, and if they don't, it's their problem to figure out. This goes unspoken. It's not fair. It's a double standard. But it's the reality. So while we continue to wait for society to shift toward equality, this chapter will equip you with tools to manage your life right now. Take control of your life and feel empowered in the workplace.

LET YOUR VALUES LEAD

My friend Harriet Shakir, an IBM executive, knows what it means to let your values lead: "In 2003, I was introduced to co-active coaching. Through a very powerful visioning exercise, I was able to see how I wanted to live my life. Sadly and surprisingly, how I was actually living did not align with my vision. Through a values exercise, I was able to uncover *my true values*, what was at my core and in my soul—not the values that I intellectually *wanted* to be mine, nor the values my parents had drummed into me. The next step was to take actions that were in alignment with those true core values that allowed me to live

Continued

my life in pursuit of my vision. My values have served as my guideposts for each major decision I've had to make. They've helped me push back on the things that seem 'good at a glance' or 'good on paper' but just weren't right for me. When I was offered a relocation that would grow my career, I measured it against both my vision and my values and made the best decision for my son and me. When a promotion was offered that would have had me flying all over the world, as a single mom, during a time when my son was entering high school and trying out for the football team, I measured it against my vision and values. I had a remarkable epiphany: I realized my career and mothering my son ran parallel to each other. There was always going to be a give and take between them, one way or another. As he grew older and started to need a different style of mothering, my career was able to grow similarly. I was able to become a different type of employee and take on different assignments that wouldn't have been aligned with one or more values years earlier. The right balance, for me, has been achieved by daring to know who I really am at my core, being strong enough to accept and love myself, and then letting that knowledge guide my actions. Life became easier, even amidst the increased pressures and stress. My path is clearer!"

Our glasses are leaking. We accept it. And yet, we've all known women who seem to have it all together—women on top of their game in their careers who have meaningful relationships, exude confidence, and even have time for exercise. So how do these women pull it off if their glasses are leaking too? Discipline and organization are part of it, to be sure. But getting everything you want out of life is also about unhooking yourself from the self-perpetuating cycle of trying to do it all. It's about being mindful of not getting lost in tasks and issues that aren't important to you.

Shelly Lazarus, chairman emeritus of Ogilvy & Mather, one of the largest marketing communication companies in the world, spoke candidly to a recent women's summit in New York City. "Be in a job you love. You can fit anything in your life that you love. Working women are comfortable failing. We are always disappointing someone . . . whether it's someone at work or our children. You must accept that we are not perfect human beings, and life, especially for women, is a series of choices. For me, having it all meant juggling . . . Were my kids always dressed neatly? No. Did they get haircuts on time? No. Was my house always clean? No. But who cares? Doing it all perfectly is perfectly impossible. Accept that, and you are much more free to enjoy the whole thing."

Lesson learned: If you make a choice that supports your current values and what you love, it's a choice you won't regret. Unless you understand what your values are, you won't be committed to understanding the Unspoken Code. There are too many tough days in business. When you put more value on the small things that don't get done on the home front rather than the big picture of what does get done in your career, you're putting unnecessary stress on yourself.

What's Important to *You*?

My friend Marie Remboulis, the head of communications of Thales Avionics, a large Fortune 500 company in Los Angeles, California, believes that every choice we make in life comes at a cost, and you set your course in life based on what you are prepared to pay. "I come from a family of immigrants who chose to leave a place where they were very comfortable because they knew it was not going to last. Freedom was precarious, and they wanted to bring up a family in a world were there would be a future, where everything was possible. As the eldest of three, I felt I had a responsibility to prove them right: I owed it to myself and my parents.

"My dad described me as perseverant. I never chose the easiest path, and once I chose, I was prepared to work hard—very hard—to achieve what I wanted. No regrets, no complaints, just happiness, because I chose it. Whether it was about school, learning another language, career choices, relationships, values, and so on, I believe once you make a choice and are prepared for what it might cost, then you are true to yourself and can truly live life to its fullest every day—the ultimate freedom!

"No matter the ups and downs, the ebbs and flows, the

successes and failures, for me it's about setting the course and pursuing it with intent. That course may change; success may be defined differently, and that is okay because we change. We learn from our mistakes and get better every day because of that."

Success, then, comes once our values are crystal clear and we can make decisions based on upholding them. Aligning your values with the career sacrifices you must make keeps stress to a minimum and success to a maximum.

What's most important to you? Is it your career? Your family? Your health? Earning a good living? All of the above? Nobody can answer this question but you. Determine what you value, because that's where success begins and ends.

ALIGNING YOUR VALUES: A WORKBOOK

List the ten things that are most important to you (e.g., children, parents, entertaining, exercise, work, religion, charity, hiking, etc.).

1. _____

2. _____

3. _____

4. _____

5. _____

6. _____

Continued

7. _____

8. _____

9. _____

10. _____

Next, rearrange in order of importance—one through ten—one being most important and ten being least important of these.

1. _____

2. _____

3. _____

4. _____

5. _____

6. _____

7. _____

8. _____

9. _____

10. _____

Now look at the top five and let these be your guide toward clarifying your personal value system. Values one through five are non-negotiable, while six through ten are areas you can weave in and out as time allows.

If you accept a new position requiring weekly travel, for example, and you have dependent family members, do you have the right help and support? If not, your stress levels could become overwhelming, causing a breakdown in both your personal and professional lives. Be honest with yourself before you say "yes" or you may be sabotaging your future success and happiness.

Perfection doesn't exist, but getting crystal clear on your values by using this guide will help you form a way of life in which you are comfortable and successful in reaching your goals, with no regrets.

Effective Time Management

Our values keep us focused and motivated. But without effective time management strategies, we run the risk of letting those values fall by the wayside. Prioritizing our values is only the first step toward success. We need to practice effective time management strategies in order to give each of those values the time and energy they deserve. For most working women, multitasking is the default mode of time management. If we have five minutes, we'll try to get two things done.

It turns out, there's a scientific reason behind this inclination:[9] Women's brains have ten times more white matter than men's brains. This white matter is the network connecting the isolated processing center that transitions from one task to the next, thus allowing the ease of transition from one task to another. Men's brains, on the other hand, have more gray matter, which helps process information, thus giving men a more single-channeled focus, or tunnel vision. (Think cavemen and the hunt for the saber-toothed tiger.)

However, while we might have the advantage when it comes to multitasking, this only serves us well when the tasks at hand don't require our full attention—like opening up mail and talking to the cable repair company.[10] The bad news is that the brain loses focus in a multitasked activity, thus ending possibly in subpar results. According to a research study coming out of Stanford University, students were divided into regular media multitaskers and non-multitaskers. In three different experiments, the multitaskers didn't do as well as the non-multitaskers.[11]

Based on this information, it might be a good rule of thumb to not multitask on jobs where your full attention is required.

9   Gregory L. Jantz, "Brain Differences Between Genders," *Psychology Today*, February 27, 2014, https://www.psychologytoday.com/blog/hope-relationships/201402/brain-differences-between-genders.

10 Eyal Ophir, Clifford Nass, and Anthony D. Wagner, "Cognitive Control in Media Multitaskers," *Proceedings of the National Academy of Sciences of the United States of America* 106, no. 37 (2009): 15583–15587, doi: 10.1073/pnas.0903620106.

11 Adam Gorlick, "Media Multitaskers Pay Mental Price, Stanford Study Shows," *Stanford News*, August 24, 2009, http://news.stanford.edu/2009/08/24/multitask-research-study-082409/.

CONSIDER A "CHECK-IN" WITH YOURSELF

Life Coach Martha Beck is a best-selling author, psychologist, and monthly columnist for *O Magazine*. When answering an overscheduled woman who wrote into her column, she wrote, "For the next week, ask yourself once every few hours, 'On the day I die, will I be glad I did the thing I'm doing now?' You're probably spending large chunks of time shopping for things you don't need, talking to people you don't like, or worrying about things that you have no control over. Cut these things out, get to sleep earlier, and arise refreshed to greet the dawn."[12]

PROVEN TIME MANAGEMENT TIPS: A MASTER LIST

Martha also recommends that people spend more time doing the things that make them feel good and less time doing the things that make them feel bad. Sounds obvious, doesn't it? But many of us don't do it. For most of us, this means giving up a few commitments and not feeling guilty for doing so. You've heard the saying *can't see the forest for the trees*, meaning that you can't see the whole situation clearly because you're too closely involved. So how can you gain some perspective on where you should be spending your most precious resource—your time? Make a list according to the guidelines that follow:

---

12 Martha Beck, "6 Ways to Improve Your Life Before Saturday," *O Magazine*, http://www.oprah.com/inspiration/iyanla-vanzant-brene-brown-life-advice#ixzz4VINSfaQk.

- **Create a Capital-L List**. Most of us put our appointments on a calendar. Take this a step further by making a detailed to-do list for the next day: work, workouts, meals, family commitments, walking the dog, and even going to the grocery store. Plan your day in fifteen-minute increments by filling in the mandatory events you must attend and work you must do, then fill in the rest with other priorities. After you fill in the mandatory activities, events, and meetings, work from the bottom to the top on the time increments. If your tasks outgrow your time, pare down your list to what's manageable and determine what you will handle, what can be delegated, and what can be eliminated altogether. Taking five or ten minutes to look at your schedule in detail beforehand will save hours of wasted time on nonessentials as well as alleviate frustration from project overload. Include time in your daily schedule to complete personal tasks such as sending out birthday cards, checking in on an elderly parent, reviewing children's schoolwork, or decluttering the kitchen counter (for your own sanity). Placing importance on your personal tasks reduces stress, and knowing you have accomplished all the important things before shutting your eyes at the end of the night will help you sleep better.

- Use the **WIN technique** of famous former football coach Lou Holtz from Notre Dame: What's Important Now? In crunch time, ask yourself if what you are doing at that moment is getting you toward your goal—WIN.

- **Practice the 3 Ds**. After planning your day using a detailed schedule, assign one of the following 3 Ds to each item: delegate, delete, do.

- **Practice the Two-One-and-None Technique**. This technique, taught by Jennifer Zientz at the Center for BrainHealth at the University of Texas, Dallas, helps you concentrate on the task at hand rather than multitasking. Perform the two most important tasks that require the highest level of thinking first: Make these non-negotiable items to complete during the workday. In addition to this, Zientz advocates taking a break to think about nothing for five minutes, five times a day; this clears your brain and leaves you feeling more relaxed.[13] Even if you can get one or two five-minute breaks, you'll find peacefulness.

- **Drop the procrastination habit**. We know that procrastination wastes time, but it's a habit, and habits can be broken. If you find yourself procrastinating, ask yourself how much you are going to regret tomorrow not having done this thing today. Assuming that tomorrow's to-do list is going to be as loaded as today's, spend the time it takes to get it done.

---

13 "How to Get More Done: Stop Multitasking," Center for BrainHealth, October 15, 2015, http://www.brainhealth.utdallas.edu/news_page/how-to-get-more-done-stop-multi-tasking.

- **Live as close as you can to the things you need**. Early in my career, I commuted forty-five minutes to and from work. One day, I got a phone call that I needed to pick my son up from childcare because he had a high fever. In a rush, driving to KinderCare, I glided through a stop sign, but not the traffic ticket. Because of this, location was one of the first things I changed about my life. Making sure that everything you need is close by can be a great stress reducer and can clear much-needed space in your daily schedule for things you value—such as a family dinner. Being home for dinner with my family has always been important to me. It's calming to put technology aside and enjoy each other's company. You may be pulling work files out after the children go to bed, but you set dinnertime aside for them. When you make proximity your goal, travel time can be replaced with things that really matter. Donna Inch, recently retired Chairman and CEO, Ford Land Development Corp. (Ford Motor Company), reflects, "It would be much more difficult to have held the positions I did at Ford Motor Company without making the decision to live and work in close proximity to the Ford Headquarters and major facilities in Dearborn, Michigan. Both myself and my husband's professional careers were in Dearborn, which allowed me to work close to where my children attended school and participated in many sports and activities. Eliminating the wasted time of commuting was key in actively balancing all aspects of our lives along with a career. If possible, I suggest managing key elements like doctors, grocer, pharmacist, hair stylist along with children's schools to be within ten to fifteen minutes from work and home. Time is just too valuable!"

- **Get the must-dos done first thing in the morning**. Brian Tracy, author of *Eat That Frog!*, suggests that you "Start with your most difficult job, or piece of the job, that gives you a jump start on the day. As a result, you'll be more energized and productive. On the days when you launch immediately into your top job, you feel better about yourself and your work than on any other day. You personally feel more powerful, more effective, more in control, and more in charge of your life than any other time."

- **Get help as soon as you can afford it**. You can't afford not to get help if you are going to advance in your career. Paying a nanny, babysitter, housekeeper, or even a high school student to run errands can help. It's an investment that will pay for itself—an investment in the business of you. Some women agonize over hiring a housekeeper or acknowledging that they could use some help. It's not your job to do everything, but it might be your job to coordinate having someone help with your household. If you're not in the financial position to do so, then delegate chores to family members. Have a family meeting, present your case, and set expectations. Once you have delegated, let that person do the task without criticizing their methods. Those towels aren't folded perfectly or the way you would do it, but at least they are done. Letting go of perfectionism makes for a happier household as well.

.....

"My theory on housework is, if the item doesn't multiply, smell, catch on fire or block the refrigerator door, let it be. No one cares. Why should you?"

−ERMA BOMBECK

- **Small, simple lifestyle changes can save lots of time**. A pick-up and drop-off dry cleaning service saves about twenty minutes a week. Picking up precooked meals also saves time. These days, you can even have your groceries delivered. Make repeat purchases on Amazon—paper products to shampoo and dog food. Autopay your bills and get all financial statements online. These are all small things you can do that will add up to save you a lot of time.

- **If you have children, have a care provider backup plan**. If you need to be somewhere for work, then you need to be there. It's unprofessional to cancel at the last minute, and moms risk this simply by being moms. Children get sick, schools close, weather happens. When it comes to childcare, don't just have a plan A but also have plans B, C, and D in case something falls through so you're not scrambling through your contacts at the last minute. Don't miss an important meeting or be distracted at work because the babysitter canceled. Know your children are being well cared for with comfortable arrangements.

- **Track your time**. We waste time without even being aware of it. We get home, have ten minutes to spare, and start pulling up emails, LinkedIn, Facebook, Instagram, or our friends' must-see YouTube links. Before you know it, you've wasted thirty minutes or more on things that certainly didn't make your "top five values" list. "Our brains are on overload with information. We are exposed to more information in a week than people in the early 1900s were in their whole lifetime," says Dr. Sandra Bond, chairman and director of the Center for BrainHealth at the University of Texas. "We're literally building an ADHD brain by jumping back and forth through our technology; there's too much shifting." The result can be increased levels of stress hormones, feeling unimportant, having trouble thinking deeply, and the inability to stay focused. This doesn't mean you have to disconnect from all electronics, but set time limits on activities you tend to waste time on. Keep personal calls to a minimum and give yourself permission to let some calls go to voice mail if they are disrupting your train of thought or the caller ID indicates that it's someone who usually calls with a litany of complaints. Shorten your emails. Decide beforehand how much time you'd like to spend on an activity and stop when you hit that limit. Be cognizant of creating your efficiency. You'll be amazed at how much time you'll free up by simply taking control of your distractions.

·····

"Respect your efforts, respect yourself. Self-respect leads to self-discipline. When you have both firmly under your belt, that is real power."

—CLINT EASTWOOD

- **Keep it low-key**. Avoid making personal appearance more complicated than it needs to be. Keep a hairstyle that fits a busy schedule. Lay out clothing, shoes, and jewelry the night before, and have your hair products, makeup, and lotions ready to go if you know you'll be pressed for time on an extra-early day. Simplifying your morning routine is a gift you can give yourself.

- **Keep your full schedule in one place**. Combine your business, personal, and family calendars in one central place at home that is accessible to everyone. This will help ensure you don't double-book yourself. Include due dates of school projects and all other commitments. The big picture of where everyone has to be will lead to adequate planning and, when necessary, plenty of time for alternative arrangements.

- **Get comfortable saying no.** Warren Buffett once said, "The difference between successful people and really successful people is that really successful people say no to almost everything." Women often struggle to say no. To break the habit of overcommitting yourself, sometimes it's easier to delay your response. When someone asks you to get involved with a project that you're not sure you have time for, say, "That sounds interesting. I'll get back to you." This gives you time to check your schedule and be comfortable with your decision. If you are faced with a difficult decision, choose the option you'll be less likely to regret, and don't look back.

- **Take time for yourself.** When we take time for ourselves, we are happier, and everyone around us is happier too. Schedule your "me-time" so you don't forget about it, and do the same for date night with your partner. Exercise can be especially difficult and you may have to get up earlier to work out, even if it's just for ten minutes. Taking care of yourself has to be a priority; that's how we manage to remain strong enough to handle as much as we do.

- **Plan ahead for the little things.** When you need to be ready for something on the horizon, give yourself enough time. For example, if you have a trip coming up, a few weeks before you leave, set up a suitcase in a spare room or corner and start packing when you have an extra five or ten minutes. You'll still have some last-minute items, but for the most part, you'll be ahead of the game. The same goes for those hectic holidays. Start planning in October for the December holiday activity peaks. Doing so allows you to take advantage of the better weather, shorter lines, and early sales. Focus on being ready for the holiday your family celebrates by the first of December. Limit your commitments. When you plan ahead, you'll be better prepared both physically and mentally to enjoy yourself and the season much more.

- **Plan ahead for the big things**. Here's the hard truth: A woman who chooses to take a few years to focus less on her career to be there for her young children will fall behind the man or woman who enters the workforce focused only on advancing their career. This time out means you need to make the most of the time you have in the workforce before and afterward. If possible, establish your career before having children. Allow yourself at least three to five years to earn a great reputation as a hard worker and an up-and-coming (if not already) successful businessperson. You don't necessarily have to work a sixty-hour-plus week. Show your employer your continued value and what's in it for them. Everyone is disposable, including you, until you start bringing in a profit or become invaluable for your firm.

- **Find a company that supports you**. Another hard truth: Whether we like it or not, many workplaces are simply not built to support working moms. Managing our time would be a heck of a lot easier if they were. So far, this list has served as a comprehensive guide to help you find a work-life balance amid a professional culture that practically precludes it. Working for a company that encourages that balance is a luxury many of us don't have, but that doesn't mean we shouldn't seek it out. If motherhood is in your future, or if you are already a mother, ask the following questions of your prospective employer:

- Do they have policies that support flexible work arrangements?
- Do tenured, upper-management females have children?
- What benefits does the company offer to provide work-life balance (e.g., onsite day care, job sharing, etc.)?
- Is your direct report supportive of work-life balance? Even if the company is pro-family, if your direct supervisor isn't your advocate, then it means nothing if you're not receiving support on a daily basis. This goes back to letting your values lead in working for an organization that supports career women with families.
- Do tenured, upper-management males have stay-at-home spouses or life partners or do they understand the busyness of a working spouse or life partner, especially if they have children at home?

A NOTE FOR WORKING MOMS

.....

"I have yet to hear a man ask for advice on how to combine marriage and a career."

−GLORIA STEINEM

Mothers with careers are dealing with unique difficulties: the extra demands of a multifaceted life. These challenges require strategic decision making about what changes you are or are not willing to make concerning your family and your career. Women are strong and resilient. There's no doubt juggling a career and a family can be done and done well. On your list of priorities, some things will fall off for a while. Think bigger picture. No one will remember missing the small details of life. What your children will remember is that you were happy and they were well cared for to the best of your abilities.

If your company is going to be open to a flexible schedule, demonstrate your loyalty. Have a well-laid-out plan. Be clear about what your optimal work arrangement will look like. What responsibilities will you handle? What might you find difficult to handle? If you're planning on becoming a mother soon, propose solutions on how your workload can be managed in your absence, knowing this may affect a number of employees. What's the time frame? Find and highlight the benefits your employer will gain from giving you what you need to achieve work-life balance. Make it easy for them to say yes.

I remember like it was yesterday how stressful it was to juggle my new career with being a single mom. May all independent career moms have a place in heaven with grapes being tossed in their mouths and foot rubs being given by anyone who doesn't show compassion for them while on this earth.

By the time I remarried and was expecting my daughter, I had already proven myself to my employer. Wanting to continue with my career, but not wanting to work the same hours as I had while building my career, I needed more flexibility. When I talked to my boss about it, I proposed my plan to complete a two-year advanced certification degree in financial planning while working ten hours a week from home and fifteen in the office. I outlined the benefits of added professional development for our clientele and worked out an arrangement whereby I would have a business phone at home. If I didn't answer by the third ring, my office assistant would pick it up. Because my employer worked with me, I became an even more loyal employee, and it greatly benefited both my personal life and career.

Before you think I had the perfect scenario and I can't relate to what you're going through, this was the same manager who sexually harassed me three years before. I pushed him away and sternly blew him off. I think this was his twisted way of repaying me for his behaving so unprofessionally and me not calling him out on it. I moved forward and on. Back then, we didn't have a lot of options. It gave me another reason to burn rubber on the road to success.

Remember: In business, everything is negotiable, so don't be shy. Get creative. The worst thing that can happen is that you are turned down—and then you can propose plan B. The most important thing is to be proactive about this life change.

.....

"Acceptance is not submission; it is acknowledgment of the facts of a situation . . . then deciding what you're going to do about it."

−KATHLEEN CASEY THEISEN

The Glass Is Half Full

Yes, your glass may be leaking, and balancing life's demands is stressful sometimes. But in the words of Billie Jean King, the tennis icon who famously beat Bobby Riggs in the Battle of the Sexes, "Stress is a privilege."

It results from the responsibilities that come with career, family, and a full life. When you're stressed out, look at the situation from a different angle. When your glass is leaking, it really means that your life is wonderfully full.

What Is No One Telling You?

THINGS TO REMEMBER . . .

- Spend some time figuring out what you value most. Then let those values guide both your personal and professional decisions.

- Be a master of time management by creating a daily to-do list. Remember the acronym WIN!

- Practice the three Ds: delegate, delete, and do. Let the rest go. Guilt is wasted energy.

- Cut out wasted time in the car by keeping your personal appointments close to your work-home route.

- Get comfortable saying, "No thank you, my plate is currently overfilled" to requests for obligations outside of home and work.

PLAN OF ACTION

As a result of what I learned in chapter 2, I am going to

Stop doing—

- _____

- _____

Start doing–

- _____

- _____

Continue doing–

- _____

- _____

Chapter Three

put on your own oxygen mask first: taking care of you

.....

*"Self-care is not selfish. You cannot serve
from an empty vessel."*

—ELEANOR BROWNN

As women, we tend to take care of everything and everyone but ourselves. When our feet hit the floor in the morning, we are often running around, tending to this and that, until we collapse in bed that night. Stress is part of life, especially when you have a career, family, and other responsibilities. But we can't let it control our lives. We have to preserve ourselves if we want to accomplish everything and maintain balance.

Your physical health depends on your ability to manage stress. Stress can be dangerous because it overworks our adrenal glands, a pair of pea-sized glands located at the top of each kidney that produce hormones in response to stress. When you spend your days tense and anxious, your adrenal glands have to work overtime, causing adrenal fatigue. Once adrenal exhaustion sets in, it's not long before the body starts experiencing chronic illness. No matter what challenges you face, you simply can't afford to live your life chronically stressed out. Something eventually has to give.

.....

"Stress reduction and mindfulness don't just make us happy and healthier. They are a proven competitive advantage."

—ARIANNA HUFFINGTON, PAST PRESIDENT AND EDITORIAL CHIEF OF *THE HUFFINGTON POST*

So, as career women, how do we handle everything? How do we take care of ourselves during life's inevitable tests and trials? How do we keep from going crazy? We build a system of stress-busting techniques that work. Stop wasting time thinking about what you *should* be doing. Feeling guilty only perpetuates the cycle of stress and takes you out of the moment. Don't let this happen any longer! The following strategies are some ways you can take care of your most important resource—you. In this chapter, you'll receive straightforward advice on how to take care of yourself so that you can set yourself up for success in your workplace environment.

My friend Susan Perlin, CPA, is an assurance partner with Plante Moran, a large accounting and consulting firm headquartered in Michigan. Sue leads her firm in their Women in Leadership initiative to attract and retain women leaders. Sue teaches her wise insights about work-life balance:

"I have found that not comparing myself to my coworkers and other partners in the firm (there is always someone who is doing better, who has done more, or who is making more money), having confidence in the lifestyle choices I've made (personally and professionally), and not worrying about what others think of me or my choices, has helped me tremendously in achieving a work-life balance and in feeling good about where I am personally and professionally. I am grateful that I work in a successful firm of very smart, professional, ethical people and that I am blessed to have choices about how much and where I work. I don't believe you can have it all. I believe everyone has choices and that to achieve happiness and balance you need to feel confident that you've made the right choices for yourself. My husband and I have become empty nesters, and I have intentionally chosen not to spend more time working. I could work more and make more money. I love my challenging career and the people I work with, but I also have other interests outside of work that bring me joy, balance, camaraderie, and stimulation. I am very satisfied with my choices."

By the end of this first section of the book, you too will have the tools and the steps enabling you to feel satisfied with your choices.

Meditate. Yes, Really.

Meditation is a practice that centers and calms the mind. By focusing your attention on breathing and letting disruptive thoughts and worries slip away, meditation gives your mind a well-deserved rest. (Even when you sleep, your restfulness can be interrupted by anxious dreams or nightmares.) It also helps you gain clarity and direction, which will help you handle your day, your job, your family, and everything else going on in your life.

The word *meditate* might make you think of sitting cross-legged and chanting. While that's certainly a method, there are others, too, such as simply closing your eyes and focusing on your breathing and nothing else for a few minutes. For readers unfamiliar with this increasingly popular practice, here are the basics: Find a quiet space where you won't be interrupted, sit in a comfortable position, and close your eyes. Then, take deep breaths from your lower abdomen, expanding your rib cage and your chest, all the way up to your throat as you inhale, breathing in and then exhaling out through your nose. You can also purse your lips and exhale slowly. Thoughts are going to enter your mind, especially when you're new to meditation. Acknowledge these thoughts and then release them. You can do this for as little or as long as you like.

Countless scientific studies prove that meditation lowers stress and improves cognitive function, creative thinking, and productivity. It even helps improve physical health.

When your brain is spinning in a million different directions or you are distracted and your mind is somewhere else, meditation restores focus and provides energy to tackle the next item on your plate. Meditation is a gift you give yourself: It provides a peace of mind that will help you more effectively live in the moment.

Albert Einstein, Benjamin Franklin, Bill Ford, Oprah Winfrey, Hugh Jackman, Robin Roberts, Bill Clinton, Clint Eastwood, Ellen DeGeneres, Paul McCartney, Tina Turner, Dr. Oz, and Richard Gere, the list goes on and on, have all been known to meditate. Google, AOL, and Apple corporations even offer meditation classes to their employees. Ray Dalio, founder of Bridgewater Associates, one of the world's largest hedge funds, said, "Meditation, more than anything in my life, was the biggest ingredient of whatever success I've had."

These successful people meditate because it works. Even a consistent five-minute meditation practice yields results. If necessary, hide out in the bathroom and shut the door if that's what it takes to build five minutes of "me-time" into your daily routine. What people discover is that meditating for five minutes is so beneficial that they slowly increase their daily commitment. As this practice becomes increasingly more widespread throughout the country, the number of resources for meditating expands. Take advantage of them! There are a number of meditation guides and timer apps you can use right on your phone. You simply adjust the time to as long as you need and a chime will signal when the time has been met. You can also check out websites, such as www.insightmeditation-center.com, www.tm.org (my practice), or www.chopra.com, which offer meaningful and well-guided meditation practices. I encourage you to keep an open mind as you look through these resources.

THE TEN BREATHS TECHNIQUE

If you are in the middle of your day in a stressful situation and can't step away for a quiet and uninterrupted five minutes, you can take ten full breaths, breathing slowly in, expanding your belly and rib cage as you inhale, then exhaling slowly. You can say the word *om* to yourself, which means peace, to remind you to clear your thoughts and create a blank slate.

You can't completely stop thoughts for long, but you can let your thoughts go for a while. There's no right or wrong way. It's called a *practice* for that reason. Yoga teacher Lynn Medow addressed her own struggles to meditate in her blog[14] and observed that meditation is different for everyone. She wrote, "One day my meditation may take me on a walk or a run, stopping in the middle of the day to eat a meal in silence, moving

---

14 www.yogabydesign.us.

in meditation through a yoga practice, or sitting in meditation in the early a.m. or late p.m."

Making the conscious effort to clear your mind and allowing yourself to be still is what's most important. The more you bring this into your daily practice, the longer you'll want to meditate. It even improves your physical health. In his book *Mind Over Back Pain*, Dr. John Sarno, professor of clinical rehabilitation medicine at the New York University School of Medicine, talks about the importance of releasing tension and how anxiety and repressed anger trigger muscle spasms, causing many of our ailments. During meditation, you feel the release of tension you didn't even know you had. It melts away and you're left wondering why you haven't meditated all your life. Your brain and body will thank you.

EMBRACING YOUR SPIRITUAL SIDE

Rarely has anyone reached their goals or found success without some kind of spiritual practice. Whatever their beliefs, they have something that settles them, and they integrate that into their routine, like going to a place of worship every week, starting their mornings off with prayer, meditation, or whatever they do to commune with their higher power. The practice is what makes spirituality powerful. In the November 2014 issue of her magazine, Oprah wrote in her "What I Know For Sure" column:

Continued

"Having enough time to give everybody who needs you and having any left for yourself is a constant struggle. But in the long run, designing space for you is the only way you can survive without burnout and resentment. There's no life without a spiritual life, and spirituality is like a muscle. It must be fueled. Fuel yourself with beauty, inspiration, music, laughter, nature, a hot soaking bath, silence. Whatever form it takes for you. Know this for sure: You have more to give when your own tank is full."

Get Physical

There is an evening hot yoga class I like to go to that consists of mostly athletic female executives coming straight from the office. One night, I had forgotten my change of clothes. It had been a very stressful day. I didn't care. I wore my expensive St. John's dry-clean-only knit suit pants and knit camisole into class. My buddies took one look at me and said, "What the heck are you doing?" I said, "I need the class. I don't care." They all burst out laughing because they could relate.

It's a known fact that exercise is important for your physical and mental health. Researchers at the University of Copenhagen conducted a study on how duration of exercise affects people. The study showed people who exercised for sixty minutes a day, thirty minutes a day, and not at all. It found that the people who exercised thirty minutes a day had as much muscle tone and were experiencing even more benefits than the people who exercised sixty minutes a day—another time saver.[15]

Some days you won't have time for thirty minutes of exercise, but you can still find five minutes to do something most days. When we fit in just five minutes of exercise, it has a positive effect on our image and our personal outlook for the rest of the day. Within minutes of getting moving, your brain lights up like a neon sign, says brain chemistry researcher David Glass, PhD, a professor in the Department of Biological Sciences at Kent State University. First comes a rush of serotonin and dopamine, the feel-good hormones that also improve memory and learning. "It sets off your reward circuitry," says Glass. "That's what makes exercise rewarding and possibly addictive."

Instead of checking your emails first thing in the morning, take a ten-minute walk or run. Do lunges, sit-ups, squats, push-ups, leg-raises, triceps, dips, or crunches. Do a plank for thirty seconds. Do four exercises, three sets of each, and get a mini workout. It's better than no workout, and being fit boosts confidence, focus, and energy. Here are some tips that will help you find ways to integrate this self-care technique into your life:

- Check out virtual apps, such as VIDA, for online coaching for a professionally tailored, motivating workout program, whether you have ten minutes a day or an hour.

---

15 University of Copenhagen, "30 Minutes of Daily Exercise Does the Trick: Same Effect in Half the Time," *Science Daily*, August 22, 2012, https://www.sciencedaily.com/releases/2012/08/120822125028.htm#.WEDkAoFXMo8.email.

- Take a virtual online toning class from your iPad that fits into your schedule.

- Use the discipline of a weekly exercise class. When people know you have a yoga or spinning class at a specific time, *you condition them* to not ask you for things at those times.

- Monitor your activity by a Fitbit or similar device. Take the stairs. Park in the back of the parking lot. Take the children for a walk around the neighborhood. Drop your child off at practice before his or her baseball game and walk or run around the park before sitting down to watch them play. As my friend Susan Peabody tells me, "Marja, you can never stop working out if you want to maintain a quality physical life. Is it always easy? No! It'd be called *playout* if it was easy. They call it *workout* for a reason! But it's your best bet for enjoying life in the long run."

Exercise is a stress buster. Figure out what works for you, and stick to it. Your body will thank you.

Be Grateful

.....

"Things turn out for people who make the
best of the way things turn out."

–JOHN WOODEN

Sandra Stilwell is a self-made business owner living in Florida. She owns ten businesses, seven of which are restaurants. (The restaurant business is primarily male dominated.) Sandra not only runs the businesses herself, she also manages, designs, and markets for the businesses as well. She knows better than anyone the importance of staying grateful.

"The most defining time in my life was August 13, 2004. Until that day, my life on Captiva Island was blissful. I had just purchased another home on the water, on Sanibel Island, and had finished building a shopping center. My restaurants were all doing well. Back then, I only had four restaurants and my small bed-and-breakfast. Category 4 Hurricane Charley was en route to hit Tampa, three hours north of us, when it suddenly made an extreme right turn directly for us. I didn't have time to evacuate, and the storm hit us head-on. We didn't have power for four weeks and no water for a week. We had no phone service of any kind. There was not one leaf on any tree; they were stripped down to the stems or were flattened.

"Everything that I owned was broken or ruined. I had generators running to keep what food could be salvaged, and I cooked for the National Guard stationed on the island, as well as other people on the island. The Salvation Army and Red Cross came out to help, and we were finally able to get ice and bottled water.

"My biggest customer base came from the large South Seas Island Resort nearby. They said they would be open by December. I rushed to get the restaurants open by then. The resort announced four different dates and eventually opened two years later. I had a lot of staff who depended on me for their livelihood, including entertainers. We opened up restaurants one by one. We had music playing and offered refuge for those wanting to observe the destruction that had taken place on Captiva, including homeowners with their insurance agents to assess the damage. Sometimes the entertainers were playing to the birds because there were very few customers actually staying on the island, but together we formed a team and a strategy and stuck with it. I never gave up, and my staff never gave up on me.

"Once the resort opened again, my charge cards were almost maxed out. I breathed a huge sigh of relief. I'll never forget the lessons that I learned from Charley. In hindsight, if I had the ability to turn that storm away, I wouldn't do it. It taught me the importance of being grateful and working through circumstances despite all odds."

Having an attitude of gratitude can change your life. Whatever your circumstances, be grateful, because there's always someone who will trade their circumstances for yours. Even if you're kicked to the curb, have gratitude for the things you do have. Instead of being angry at the world, say, "Great, curb, now what am I supposed to learn from this?"

Tap into Your Inner Strength

Although I was born in the United States, I am 100 percent Finnish—thus my name: Marja Liisa (pronounced "Mar-ya Leesa"). Finnish people live their lives abiding by *sisu*, a fundamental and defining concept of their culture. Although the term cannot be directly translated, it loosely means strength, resilience, determination, and perseverance. It means "grit." Envision sisu as a circle of faith, like a wheel. Think of these many terms as spokes. This circle of faith keeps you moving forward, as challenging as life may become. The strength of sisu within you is much stronger than the adversities surrounding you. As one Finland university proudly writes on the homepage of their website, "Sisu is not momentary courage . . . it is the ability to sustain that courage."[16]At its core, sisu is about maintaining an inner strength that gets you through the day.

---

16 http://www.finlandia.edu/about/our-finnish-heritage/.

Like many Finns, sisu has guided me through trying times. It helped me cope with living on the other side of the world in Korea to making my exit strategy from an abusive marriage, despite having no money, no car, and a child. And I believe it can help you, too, in countless situations. As a centering force, sisu can help you remain calm in trying situations and can help you move forward rationally, instead of emotionally—a critical component in any business professional. There is an unspoken energy in being able to harness a power that comes from within and use it to your advantage. Practice this in your daily life—the next time someone says something can't be done or challenges you on a point you're trying to make, practice being centered and calm and remember that with this inner strength, you are as powerful as every man (and woman!) in the room.

SHE DARED TO PUSH THROUGH

Sisu (pronounced see-soo) has a long tradition of strength. Finnish women are known for their personal and professional strength. My aunt, Dr. Amy Kaukonen, was an inspiration to me and exemplifies this strength. Amy finished first in her class in high school as well as at the Women's Medical College of Philadelphia. After school, she started practicing medicine in Fairport Harbor, Ohio, in 1920. Witnessing many medical maladies associated with the whiskey runners, moonshiners, and the rowdy public at large, it was no surprise that Amy became a staunch opponent of alcohol and the dance halls and corrupt government of the Fairport Community. Her public views attracted the attention of Fairport Harbor's Kasvi Temperance Hall. She was approached by the Peoples Reform Party and, benefiting from the recently passed Nineteenth Amendment, she became a candidate for public office. In 1921, Amy beat her mayoral opponent. History was made.

Once in office, Mayor Kaukonen waged a battle with a reelected marshal, J. H. Werbeach, who ignored Fairport's bootlegging activities. Threats were made against her, and one man attacked her in her office, giving her a black eye. Two tumultuous years followed. Werbeach's sudden death in 1923 allowed her to appoint Leander Congos as the new marshal, which led to positive changes. She revoked alcohol permits, jailed bootleggers, and promoted bootleg eradication plans in the village. In 1922, she used the Homeland Security provisions of the era to issue mayor's warrants to search for violations. She received accolades in New York, Cleveland, Columbus, and Boston—President Warren Harding even sent her an appreciation letter and two Airedales for protection. After decades of corruption and illegal dock activities, her civic policies led to paved streets and a water, fire, and police service. New and improved public schools were established, and Fairport transformed into a leading industrial power of the twentieth century. Dr. Kaukonen continued to deliver babies and maintain her private practice throughout this transformation.

Amy's spunk and tenacity spread throughout the country, and she received numerous marriage proposals. A gentleman from New York City sent a proposal on a Sunday

Continued

via telegraph, stating if Amy didn't accept his proposal by Thursday, he'd jump off the Brooklyn Bridge. Amy cleverly replied, "Why wait until Thursday?" Dr. Amy returned to her medical practice after accomplishing her goals during prohibition.

Amy could have easily caved to the violence she faced. Instead, she stood tall, practiced sisu, and turned Fairport Harbor into a productive city. She did it well.[17]

You have what it takes to succeed. In the business world, you will be challenged frequently. I offer the term sisu for you to make it a part of yourself, like I did. Deposit it into your heart. When life gets tough, pull sisu out. When you want to quit, keep plowing through. Internalize the concepts of perseverance, endurance, bravery, inner strength, and tenacity. Tap into your own frontier heroes, like Amy. Continue to carry the torch on their behalf, widening the tough, dusty, and challenging path they cleared for us today. How are you going to be the hero for your future sisters?

---

17 Biographical information on Amy Kaukonen sourced from Lasse O. Hiltunen, "American Finn Leaves Legacy: The Dr. Amy Kaukonen Story," Finnish Heritage Museum, December 2007, http://finnishheritagemuseum.org/AAArchive/Featured%20Stories/Kaukonen/index.html.

Live in the Present

.....

*"The past, I think, has helped me appreciate the
present—and I don't want to spoil any of it by
fretting about the future."*

−AUDREY HEPBURN

Whatever discord you are experiencing personally or professionally in any given moment, know *it's not happening to
you*. It's happening *around you* and it's happening *for you*. The
chaos is outside of you. Simply recentering your mindset can
help you learn what you can from it. To do this, take a walk
outside, even if it's just for a few minutes. Take in the scen-
ery. Appreciating the present puts life into perspective and can
help you detach yourself from worries about the future that
likely will never come to fruition.

It's about perception. You alone have the strength and ability to shift your perception, as everything we do is a choice.
As discussed in chapter one, you can choose to be frustrated,
angry, and grumpy or grateful, content, and pleasant. Take
note of negative thoughts or emotions and ask yourself, "Will
it even matter five years from now?" The answer, likely, will be
no. In fact, it probably won't matter next week or a single day
from now.

We've discussed how scientists have shown that multitasking decreases overall effectiveness. When you're spending

time with your children, be present—not on the phone, reading emails, or checking media sites. If you're talking to your companion, be focused 100 percent on what the person has to say—not on all the things that you have to do. Quality time is the greatest gift you can give. Giving yourself the tools to live in the present moment, instead of living in fear and worrying about the future, will set you up for success in the workplace by helping you refocus on what's most important.

More Ways to Beat Stress

- Do your best to get enough sleep. How many hours do you sleep without the alarm clock? That's how much sleep you need. Arianna Huffington's book *The Sleep Revolution* is a great resource that discusses our dilemma of lack of sleep with supporting scientific data. We need seven to eight hours of sleep per night . . . really!

- Laugh! Talk to someone funny. Tell a joke. Find a joke. Connect with people who lift you up. Practice being good at one or two jokes. Humor connects us to people.

- Speak up. Assert yourself. Learn to say no instead of agreeing to things you don't want to do or don't have time to do and then end up feeling resentful. Speaking up builds self-confidence. That's a win-win.

- Get a massage. No time? Take a few minutes to rub your own neck and shoulders to loosen up tight muscles.

- Stretch on your own or take a yoga class. When your body feels tense, do some stretches to feel instantly renewed.

- Reflexology is the technique of applying pressure to areas of the soles of the feet that correspond with organs in your body. Reflexologists can target areas in the ball of the foot to alleviate stress. Keep a roller under your desk. Roll it against the sole of your foot, releasing those tight tendons.

- Eat a diet of unprocessed food and natural drinks, including water, tea, and wine (in moderation, of course). Limit preservatives, chemicals, processed foods, and meats to the best of your ability.

- Take long, deep breaths instead of shallow ones. Best-selling holistic health author Dr. Andrew Weil recommends the 4-7-8 Breath for stress relief. Start by exhaling through your mouth, making a whooshing sound, and empty all the air out. Then inhale for a count of four, hold your breath for a count of seven, and then exhale through your mouth for a count of eight. Weil recommends doing four of these breathing exercises twice daily.

- Prepare in advance for how you will react in stressful situations. This tip came from an article in the July 2014 issue of *O Magazine* that described stress management strategies used by Navy SEALS.

When you are facing a situation that you know could be potentially stressful, like your boss calling you into the office or a meeting with an upset client, take a few minutes to *mentally run through the likely scenarios* of what might unfold and how you can optimally react. This dress rehearsal works well to make you be and feel more prepared—thereby helping to significantly reduce anxiety.

Embracing "The Suck." When faced with a tough situation, instead of giving up, embrace it as an opportunity to surpass your competitors. "It's one thing to be an excellent athlete when the conditions are perfect," Lu Lastra, director of mentorship for Naval Special Warfare and a former SEAL command master chief, told *O*. "But when the circumstances aren't so favorable, those who have stronger wills are more likely to rise to victory. Bring on the storm to give you the opportunity to see what you are made of."

- Call for a nontechnology night. Make dinnertime cell phone, technology, and television-free.

You Can Handle Everything That Comes Your Way

In the beginning of my career, a visiting wholesaler came into my office and shared some advice about lightening up. Of course, at the moment, I was offended. But he was right. I was too tense. Stressful situations are part of life, but *you control how you respond*. Learning how to manage stress with exercise, meditation, spirituality, and healthy living keeps you more centered. It improves your focus. Every day you'll improve at reacting with thought and intention rather than emotion. You may find yourself lightening up instead of being so serious about everything, and as a result, you may find life is more enjoyable. Incorporating some of these stress management strategies into your life will give you the power to enjoy each day to its fullest.

What Is No One Telling You?

THINGS TO REMEMBER . . .

- Tap into the power of sisu: inner strength, guts, stamina, preservation, and that indomitable spirit.
- Meditate daily: It changes your outlook on life and keeps you centered throughout the day.

- Take care of your body, even when you're slammed, by fitting in a short workout.

- Reduce stress throughout the day by releasing tension. Pay attention to your body. Breathe deep and relax your shoulders.

- Embrace tough situations as opportunities to surpass your competitors. The end result of being good or being great by that little effort will put you at the top.

PLAN OF ACTION

As a result of what I learned in chapter 3, I am going to

Stop doing–

- _____

- _____

Start doing–

- _____

- _____

Continue doing–

- _____

- _____

PART TWO

Becoming
an Office
Power Player

Chapter Four

how to play ball with men

.....

"You have to learn the rules of the game. And then you have to play better than anyone else."

—ALBERT EINSTEIN

Men and women speak different languages. Sometimes you say things to men and their response makes it obvious that they're *not* on the same page. Men and women think differently, our brains are wired differently, and we see the world from different perspectives. As an example, in the business world, we often observe that men focus on the outcome or conclusion, whereas women are often more detail oriented and dedicated to the process. These differences can cause conflict and require different approaches. Despite our differences, men and women must work together effectively in the corporate world to get things done. This means staying receptive when hearing uncomfortable feelings from each other without attacking, judging, or rushing in to try to "fix" it. It means leaning in with more conversations, not less.

I've learned to see and understand these differences in my relationship with my husband and business partner. Jerry, with his alpha personality, gets bored quickly. In meetings with our colleagues, he used to become impatient and run over what I was saying to speed things up. He meant no disrespect: He just wanted me to get to the point—the bottom line. I felt his behavior *was* a form of disrespect, but I used to allow it to happen. I hate to admit that I didn't speak up at times when I was challenged by a strong personality. Instead of regrouping with knowledge and confidence, I receded. I knew better. I felt I was sabotaging myself, and afterward, I felt shame for not allowing my voice to be heard.

I was lucky enough to work with my business coach on these critical communication issues, and he taught me a valuable lesson: When you have the opportunity to assert yourself, don't second-guess yourself. Think through what you want to say so you stay focused. If not now, when? Every time you do, it will give you more confidence. Eventually, I was able to shift my attitude and behavior, as will other women who wish to grow. The ABCs don't stop at any point as you increase your responsibility in your career. As you become stronger, with more experience and wisdom under your belt, you'll become more focused on obtaining the results you need from negotiations.

There are always three ways to look at things—your perception, my perception, and the reality. Instead of valuing what we both brought to the table and accepting our differences, we were unaccepting of those differences. Had we continued to be narrow-minded, we both would have lost out—and the client experience would have been less than ideal. It was therefore up to us to define our roles in a team setting, as partners with different roles, rather than competing to fill the same roles. So we had to get over the power struggle, the tug-of-war, by both of us dropping the ropes. Periodically, we'd both try another game of tug-of-war, until one of us again laid down the rope, knowing it would end up in a stalemate and waste of valuable time. We kept our focus on the end goal: our business plan. Three plus three equals six. Two plus four also equals six. Understanding we have the same end goal in mind but can get there using different approaches makes us both right.

The higher you go in the corporate world, the more alpha males, and alpha females for that matter, you'll encounter. The sooner you learn how to play ball with those individuals, the faster and smoother your climb will be. This chapter will introduce you to the Unspoken Code and help you navigate these alpha personalities with ease.

THE IMPORTANCE OF MENTORSHIP

Regularly speaking with a woman who understands gender issues and is experienced enough to give advice on how to handle situations can be a critical asset in understanding the Unspoken Code and climbing the corporate

Continued

ladder. Female mentors build our confidence that we, too, can press through challenging circumstances. Find women in your industry to partner with. Informally invite similarly positioned women in your office or industry to go out for a nonbusiness dinner. With your schedules, it may only happen twice a year, but it's a great way to connect and build camaraderie.

However, don't limit yourself to finding female-only mentors. In speaking with other female executives, all have said it's equally important to have a male mentor for several reasons. One, they may be the highest up in your organization or other organizations you may be considering. Two, advice from a male's point of view can sometimes be the missing link to getting ahead.

Finding a mentor may appear daunting, but understand it is part of most business cultures. Some companies formalize a mentoring program for their employees. The secret to finding a good mentor is to understand what it is you're looking for and whether or not a potential mentor is a good fit for what you need. When looking for a mentor, ask yourself, "Is this person bold enough to be honest with me?" If they can't be candid, they're not going to be helpful. Choose someone who can be objective and direct with you, yet who'll have patience when you make mistakes—one you'll have no fear of recourse from. For this reason, it may be best to choose someone besides your boss (who has a personal stake in your performance). The mentoring relationship has a different dynamic and focuses on the big picture of your success. Following are six tips to help you find success as a mentee.

1. **Have an idea what you want to be mentored on.** Make an honest assessment of your strengths and weaknesses. What are the Unspoken Codes you want to decipher in your particular field? What road-blocks are you hitting? Make a list of the top two or three issues and bring these to your mentor meeting to ensure you are prepared to get the most value from their limited time.

2. **Be punctual.** Know that your mentor is busy and carving out time to help you. Don't let them regret the obligation. Keep it light. Ask them what times work best for them and don't extend the time. Position it as a periodic inspirational session for half an hour every four to six weeks, for example, unless they are sincerely offering more.

3. **Be willing to think outside the box to make the mentoring relationship work.** Drive your mentor to work or tag along on their errands one day. Do whatever it takes.

4. **Ask good questions and be a good listener.** Ask your mentor what they see in you that would be helpful to adjust for your business growth. Don't record conversations; instead, take notes you can refer to later. Ask for suggestions. Ask permission to email subsequent questions, not to exceed one or two per month.

5. **Be easy to work with.** Email your mentor before each meeting to remind them you're coming and to make sure your appointment time still works for

Continued

them. Let them know that they don't have to respond to your email unless there is a change in their schedule. The less time they have to take, the better.

6. **Offer up service in return for their time and wisdom.** What can you offer the mentor for helping you? Sometimes, seasoned individuals can use a hand on new technology. Offer to review their LinkedIn profile or assist them in navigating through new software. When you reciprocate, your mentor will see time well spent with you as more valuable and mutually beneficial.

Even if your mentor is not physically present, you can mentally call on them time and again to help you navigate tough situations by considering what they might do in your situation. I continue to strive to handle situations in a way that would have pleased my own mentor. Even without someone to guide you, you can still stretch yourself to find different perspectives on your situation. That's what being a successful mentee is all about.

Navigating the differences between the male and the female modes of working is something every woman in the workplace will deal with in her career, and it is critical to find ways to manage these situations effectively and productively. Men don't have to navigate like we do: Remember, we're the ones coming into the Super Bowl locker room, not them. It's all about the endgame. As women, to know this and understand that it's about us shifting to fit the environment, in a healthy way, of course, is imperative.

Mary Spensley, a successful businesswoman who has served as co-owner of a local franchise, SERVPRO, for fifteen years and has worked in a male-dominated field, shares the following story illustrating this point:

"One of the biggest frustrations I have is not being included in the decision-making process, although my associates consult with one another. So what's important to me and what's important to them are inherently two different things. I go out of my way to inform them so that they can make an educated decision. My recommendation is to be exceptionally organized by writing everything down, sending yourself an email as a reminder to ask about any upcoming meetings. I also recommend sending team members a request to include me in the decision-making process. Lean the heck in if you want to feel included. It's up to us to take that ball and run with it."

A big roadblock to gender equality in the workplace is how differently men and women handle confrontation and criticism from a lifetime of conditioning. Don't believe it? Stop by a high school football practice. You'll see coaches screaming at the boys and the boys just shrugging it off. Watch the girls' soccer practice on the other side of the turf. No one is screaming at them, and, if they were, there would be tears. Women take confrontation personally. We have been raised to be pleasant and acquiescent, and we need to awaken the power within.

The reality is that the business world is a man's game, and many men remain wary or uncertain about working with females. We can't wait for them to take responsibility to make those workplace relationships work for everyone. So what do we do as women to alleviate men's uncertainties about working with us? You don't have to comport yourself like a man to be successful in business. Never shy away from being the woman you are. We're all on the field playing the game. What's most important is understanding the different ways we bring ourselves to the table and adjusting accordingly.

Men Are from Mars

In his book *What Men Don't Tell Women about Business*, Christopher V. Flett reveals the man's perspective on business and working with the opposite sex. Christopher writes, "Female authors that I have read spend a lot of time giving women advice on how to move ahead in business by staying clear of the alpha male. These female authors present this avoidance tactic as their process for being successful. However, when you avoid working relationships with successful and driven individuals, any success that could have been realized is missed as well." Once you understand the other person's point of view and motivations, you can more effectively communicate and work with each other.

Working with someone means understanding what makes

that person, man or woman, tick. Analyze their personality to some degree, so you know what you're walking into in any given situation. You've probably encountered at least one of the popular workplace personalities. We all recognize the alpha male personality type. He's usually the guy in charge. Then there's the beta male, who is usually the guy who does the alpha male's work. The alpha female and beta female fit within the business structure in similar ways. Recognize and respect different personalities. Your intent is to craft your message in order to accomplish the desired result. Are you talking to an alpha male or female who values the bottom line? Or to a beta male or female who is more interested in the details than the process of reaching the bottom line? Connect with them accordingly.

We've been privy to one or more personality tests telling us how to interact with each personality. It's nearly impossible to remember all these different personalities and how you are supposed to interact with each of them when you're not dealing with this on a regular basis. Watch the person to the best of your ability. Are they alpha personalities that are short on attention span? Are they more talkative and more in touch with their emotions? Reading body language is the easiest thing to remember. If you can see a negative reaction in their face or body stature, you know you need to adjust so they can "hear" you.

My friend and fellow yoga studio regular Sue Maniloff, a business development executive in the publishing industry, discusses this issue from her own experience:

"Effective communication means speaking with an open mind and understanding how to deliver your message so your audience understands. I am a seasoned professional with an extensive background in sales, business development, and licensing. In 2014, as a director at a well-known, global industry leader in the education technology space, I was tasked with managing the organization's largest third-party, multi-million-dollar relationship, developing a proposal, obtaining the internal approvals, driving the negotiation, and ultimately closing the deal and securing the business.

"There were many layers of departments and executive management to navigate, both internally at my own organization and externally with the customer. After several months of preparation, we were at the final stages of negotiation, in an impressive (some may say intimidating) boardroom in London. There I was, with three executive men from my organization, along with three executive men from the customer side. All was going well until we hit a minor bump in the road, and all involved were myopically focused on this one small sticking point . . . with the exception of myself. I knew that if we could not move past this small point, the entire deal was at risk.

"After a few hours, I requested a brief break so I could have the chance to speak privately with my team of executives. As we stepped out of the room, I knew that I had to ask specific questions to find out what the real concern was all about, and then provide hard data to quiet their concerns. Was this point so important that it was worth losing the deal over? Are we willing to give in, in order to move forward? If not, what is the root cause of the concern? Is it because we just need to win? Is it in the best interest of the business? Is it ego? After letting them talk and listening to their valid objections, I then presented my team with hard data—metrics on the importance of this negotiation to the many products and services this deal would feed, along with securing our position in the highly competitive marketplace. Once I pulled out my iPad, with well-prepared metrics and financials, along with a few charts and graphs that I had prepared, my team regrouped, changed direction, and started to discuss ways we could compromise this point in order to move forward to successfully close the deal. And we did.

"In my experience, the best way to manage different communication styles is to understand how your audience thinks and what pushes their buttons. Anticipate the questions and pain points and push back. And most importantly, be prepared to communicate in the style that will bring the greatest results. I knew that my team would want to see numbers and charts regarding customers, competitors, products, and financials. The negotiation ended well with a long-term partnership, which was beneficial for both parties."

WE NEED TO LEARN TO WORK TOGETHER

In communicating with alpha men, Connie Glaser, a best-selling author and syndicated columnist, gives these strategies for women in her book, *GenderTalk Works*:

1. **Cut to the chase. Speak in bulleted points and sound decisive.** Focus on presenting your thoughts and ideas logically and succinctly. Root out *feeling* words and phrases and avoid hedging, tag questions, and sharing unnecessary details.

2. **Choose your words carefully. When it comes to emotional topics, men panic easily.** So, play to his conversational strengths. Don't ask him how he feels about something; ask him what he thinks about it.

3. **Speak up.** Don't allow men to interrupt you. Be firm and tell them, "I'm not finished" or "Just a minute, please."

4. **Stop saying "I'm sorry" just to be polite.** Apologize only if you're wrong.

5. **Desensitize yourself.** Learn not to take male comments and criticisms personally. Learn to separate business matters from personal feelings.

6. **Don't expect men to be mind readers.** If you want or need something, ask for it. And don't dilute comments or criticisms. Be direct—men expect this and appreciate it.

There are many pitfalls when it comes to workplace communication, and learning how to navigate them with ease and humor is an important element of learning the Unspoken Code of business. It's unspoken because most men don't understand how our brains work. They only know that they work differently. It's up to you to learn their language. Think of it as if you are going to France for the year and you don't know a bit of French. You're going to be traveling the countryside. Of course, you'll make the effort to take courses so you can navigate your way around the language as well as the roads. Why wouldn't you make the effort to understand something you're in day to day or year to year?

Men get a pass more often than females because their language is the norm. The goal is to continue to educate a diverse workplace to improve communication skills so all can be heard.

PLAYING ON THE WOMEN'S TEAM

Successful communication is critical to playing ball with men, and while I've focused mostly on how to do so with men, it is equally critical to communicate effectively with the women on your team. One of the most powerful ways to play the game is through networking with other women and talking to them about how to thrive on a male-dominated team. Build a network for women to share their challenges and successes. When you find yourself in a delicate work situation, you will be comfortable and confident because

Continued

of the knowledge you've gained from the women in your network. You'll have a cache of tools in your mind you can use to overcome frustrations. The more we hear about what to do in professional situations, and the more we associate ourselves with other women, the stronger we'll all be.

Trust Issues

Here's another hard fact about the Unspoken Code: People trust others who are like them. And yet, trust is the most important factor in productive communication. Men naturally trust other men with confidence, but they don't as readily trust women. It's extremely critical that women are aware of this in interactions with men. People's history with women, from their mother to their most recent female employee, unfortunately affects you, even though it has nothing to do with you. To break the myths of women dropping career responsibilities to take care of family, or being emotional versus factual, or worse yet, thinking you're there to satisfy the diversity mandates, this is something you need to be cognizant of.

The standard for business-appropriate communication and behavior between men and women has changed significantly over time, and it's prudent to proceed with caution. There are certain unspoken communication guidelines between genders that are important to acknowledge and understand. Women view the desire to share as a form of bonding. Men, however, often view this as a betrayal of confidence. It's important to know this and honor it when dealing with men. Therefore, on the issue of trust, it's important to consider the sensitivity of sharing confidences because men don't view it as sharing but as a betrayal.

Bob Bethoney, my husband's prior boss and friend, was a wise man who reflected on being cognizant of the consequences of saying too much: "Before sharing information, ask yourself, 'What is the real benefit of your sharing this information? To make you feel included? To make you feel better about yourself that you have a confidence to share? Is it benefiting the person you are speaking of?' If not, then it's not something to say."

The bond between businessmen can often seem impenetrable and is certainly unspoken. My friend and neighbor Kim Reese describes how she successfully navigated through her career as an air traffic controller in a male-dominated, hostile work environment:

"In 1981, President Ronald Reagan fired more than eleven thousand air traffic controllers. There was a mass hiring to replace the fired controllers, along with intensive training. I was one of those called upon to replace the fired controllers, and we were affectionately known as *scabs*. As you can imagine, this was a male-dominated industry, and women in the business were quite an anomaly. The controllers who did not go out on strike were determined to help their striking 'brothers' by making sure the scabs did not pass the initial training, which was pass or fail, therefore forcing the return of the striking controllers. If you failed, you were immediately separated—government speak for fired.

"Much of the testing was subjective, and the failure rate for scabs was 60 percent—and even higher for women scabs. I found it particularly important for me to keep my head down, not be noticed, and study as much as possible. I didn't even go home for Christmas for fear of losing valuable study time. Once assigned to an airport, the men's bathroom door, next to the elevator, was kept wide open for all passersby to see in. It was meant to be intimidating to the few women assigned—and it was. During training, we were yelled at and had plastic strips (that held flight plans) thrown at us if we made a phraseology error. Since they didn't get any reaction from me, they saw that their silly antics were not working. Or perhaps they got bored and finally stopped and became coworkers. The other women who cried and responded with emotion mostly didn't make it. It was only with undying perseverance and patience that I gained respect from my fellow male controllers."

Winning as Women

Men and women will continue to learn from and adjust to each other's strengths and contributions, but without initiative, it's not going to happen as fast as we'd like. We have everything to gain by being willing to adjust. Change has to start somewhere. And it starts with you.

As different as we are, men and women also share some fundamental similarities. We want men to recognize our strengths, just as we appreciate what men bring to the table. Both men and women are driven by insecurities on some days, feeling the opposite sex has it out for the other. On other days, we relish what we bring to the workplace. At times, we all feel like frauds. Other times, we know we have the right answer to the dilemma and we make a real difference. Sometimes, we feel like we're not good enough. And some days, our egos are forces to be reckoned with. Understanding these commonalities that unite us while respecting our unique perspectives as men and women can only make the game better.

.....

"The day will come when men will recognize woman as his peer, not only at this fireside, but in councils of the nation. Then, and not until then, will there be the perfect comradeship, the ideal union between the sexes that shall result in the highest development of the race."

—SUSAN B. ANTHONY

Playing Ball with Men: The Ultimate Playbook

Remember the analogy of playing ball with men. You're on their football field. Knowing this will help you learn to talk their talk so you can walk their walk. These tips will help you do just that.

- **Be honest and have an opinion**. People will be drawn to you for being honest. It's part of being a great leader.

- **Don't talk about your personal life much**. Know that you'll be held to higher standards than men. Don't bring up your personal life at work outside a light conversation with a close few.

- **Don't ask for affirmation from men**. Men view this as a weakness. Walk in with power and authority. You don't need *anyone's* affirmation. If you ask them their opinion, they will think you don't have a strong opinion of your own. Don't say the words *asking for your opinion* directly; use it in the context of conversation.

- **Don't gossip or bad-mouth people**. Not even once. It's a credibility killer. Respect confidentiality because it will be tested. The old saying, "If you don't have anything nice to say, don't say anything at all," is important in earning trust.

- **Avoid cliques**. Don't sit at meetings with only your female colleagues or male pals. At conferences and other events, intermingle and talk to people at all levels, from administration to executive. Take a seat at the table!

- **Don't answer your cell phone or text when you're in a conversation with someone else**. It's plain rude. Give that person your undivided attention. Some women do this more out of habit because we are often the first responders for our family. Wait until you're done with the conversation or meeting, then excuse yourself.

- **Own it**. Taking responsibility when an issue arises will go much further in reaching a quick resolution than blaming someone else. Even if it's not your fault, blaming an issue on your assistant doesn't shed a positive light on you. The buck stops with you.

- **Praise in public and criticize in private**. If someone is disrespectful to you, handle it, but don't embarrass people with negative feedback in public. Talk to them after the meeting and tell them you have zero tolerance for their behavior. Just do it in private. If it's recurring, follow proper protocol.

- **Don't be late**. When you are late for appointments, you are saying to the other person that their time is less important than yours. If you're late, apologize and move on. Don't blame it on a wardrobe malfunction or launch into a detailed explanation about a sick child. Just jump in and get up to speed on what you missed.

- **Don't offer your ideas in the form of a question**. If you want your audience to have confidence in you and what you're saying, speak with assurance. Don't raise your voice at the end of a sentence. Add value to conversations by knowing your facts. When you make a suggestion, have three reasons why it makes sense. Don't say, "Well, believe me. I know this will work." Expect to be challenged, and have your playbook answers ready.

- **Don't cry, especially in meetings**. Think about any distraction—like the national anthem or whether a favorite sports team is going to make the playoffs. If that doesn't work, excuse yourself to the restroom and return after you've collected yourself. Don't apologize. Just rejoin the meeting. Men cry on the sports field, and yes, that's okay by them. But they don't cry at work and they don't know how to handle it when you do.

- **Be helpful to your female colleagues**. We can be our own worst enemies, working to undermine and eliminate each other from the competition. But if we work to bring more women to the top of male-dominated businesses, the business world becomes more inclusive—and that's good for everyone. Hire women as often as you can, if you, in turn, want to be hired. It's good karma.

- **Don't take business personally**. Taking it personally is one of our weaknesses. Men blow things off more easily.

We need to learn from them and strive to take the emotion out of situations by responding with the facts. This is how men roll, and we can learn from that. If you falter with this, men will view it as a weakness. If you do falter, laugh about it, learn from it, and move on.

- **Proactively reach out to male colleagues**. Since golfing and cigar smoking with the boys isn't always on our priority list, don't make yourself a loner. Engage in friendly (not flirting) conversation in the work kitchen. Connect with fellow workers by proposing a question or asking their thoughts on a current business topic.

- **Keep it short**. When communicating with men, give them the headlines: fifteen words or less. If you need to give more detail, think of the first and last paragraph only and omit the paragraphs in between.

If you cultivate a calm and professional communication style, even in the midst of drama and chaos, people will remember you. The sooner we put these rules into play, the sooner we will experience abundant accomplishments.

What Is No One Telling You?

THINGS TO REMEMBER . . .

- Too often women feel intimidated walking into a group of all men. They'll take a seat against the wall of the conference room instead of at the table and stare straight ahead. Go in with confidence and, after you sit down, browse the room to acknowledge those that are there.

- Repay your mentor for their time with something that can benefit them, like sharing tips on their new phone, app, or computer.

- Be cognizant of whom you are working with. Do they have an alpha personality? Adjust your communication style so that your message can easily be understood by both men and women.

- Think of communicating with men like a news article: Give them the headlines, the facts of the first paragraph, and the summary of the last paragraph. Save the details in case they ask questions.

- Have an arsenal of women executives you can ask for advice. It will boost your confidence in handling a situation.

PLAN OF ACTION

As a result of what I learned in chapter 4, I am going to

Stop doing—

- _____

- _____

Start doing—

- _____

- _____

Continue doing—

- _____

- _____

Chapter Five

tips and scripts for communication and confrontation

.....

"You can have brilliant ideas, but if you can't get them across, your ideas won't get you anywhere."

—LEE IACOCCA

Dad was a big advocate for effective communication. He gave me a book, *Practical Voice Training*, written in the 1940s by Dr. Harriett Grim to help improve communication by using the right tone of voice. Needless to say, we've come a long way since the 1940s. Thankfully, the sound of a woman's voice is no longer her most important communication challenge. Effective communication ensures the other person hears the message you want to deliver. Being a good communicator is imperative to success.

Communication is holistic. It fully encompasses what you

feel inside and what you project on the outside. The verbal component—how you sound and what you say—contributes to the impression you create and maintain with people. You are creating a vision with your words. (The nonverbal component is equally important and will be dealt with in the next chapter.) The Unspoken Code of communication and handling confrontation is this: No one gives you a cheat sheet on what to say or how to say it. It's learned over time. In this chapter, I *am* giving you that cheat sheet. By shifting a few words, having a confident voice, and being a strong listener, you can ensure your voice will be heard.

ASSESSING YOUR VERBAL SKILLS: A REALITY CHECK

- Do you rush to get your words out, or do you take time to think before you speak?
- Do you sound articulate—clear and concise?
- Does your voice sound confident, or do people consistently ask you to speak up?

If you're having a hard time assessing these important questions, consider reaching out to someone close to you who can help you, someone who is comfortable enough to give direct and honest feedback. It is equally important to be able to not take the direct and honest feedback personally but rather as a gift. Improve where it is important to improve.

In her book *How to Say It for Women*, Phyllis Mindell, Ed. D., talks about how the Harvard Case Studies track CEO days:

> What do leaders do all day? As you progress up the career ladder, you invest ever greater portions of the day communicating. The Harvard Business Review schedule for a typical woman leader suggests that her day is roughly divided into: 20 percent reading, 20 percent writing, 40 percent formal presentations (she's also listening and speaking informally during these presentations), 30 percent in informal meetings (at which she speaks and listens while sitting). These figures add up to more than 100 percent because the communications overlap. She spends all her travel time communicating: speaking on the cell phone; reading books, proposals, and periodicals; and writing on her computer.
>
> Yet, despite the progress of the past two decades, many women have yet to generate a language that works in the executive suite. Whatever your management philosophy, whether you're a dictator, an enabler, a mentor, a drill sergeant or a coach, you'll prosper when you adopt and adapt the language of success.

Effective verbal communication exudes comfort and confidence in all personal and business relationships. Your ability to effectively communicate shouldn't depend on whom you're communicating with. Hone your skills to ensure you're at the top of your game whether you are talking to someone who is less educated or successful or meeting with your CEO.

Tip: It is helpful to bring to mind people who you respect and admire and determine how meaningful their communication style and skill is to the impression they make on you. Make them your "communication avatar," and bring them to mind as needed to keep you on your sharpest game.

Communicating Confidence

Improving verbal communication skills requires building confidence, becoming comfortable with words, and being *authentic*. The following tips will help you position yourself and your communication style to get the results you want, whether you're giving a speech, presenting at a meeting, or simply engaging in a workplace conversation.

1. PRACTICE

Speaking in front of people, whether at a presentation or in a meeting, is an inevitability in the business world, especially if you are trying to make your mark. Public speaking is an especially critical component of good communication, and it requires practice in order to master. When you speak from a prepared but partially memorized script, you can get caught up in concentrating too hard on remembering the words, instead of delivering the message, causing you to stumble and sound choppy. Your message will be lost. **When you speak from your heart, you speak with passion**. Knowing your material inside and out will ensure you won't have to think about it—you can speak deliberately, pause as needed, and enunciate certain words to enhance your message. Following the Secret of Five steps before any presentation or public speaking engagement will ensure you deliver your intended message with ease.

The Secret of Five

1. Read your talk out loud from your notes, looking up into your imaginary audience from time to time.

2. Stand in front of your imaginary audience, using index cards of your talk. Review the time it takes to deliver the talk. Check back on your full notes to see what areas you need to embrace more and which you need to cut.

3. Stand in front of your imaginary audience again, using your index cards. Mark red vertical lines where you need to pause, and underline words you need to enunciate. Look around the room. Imagine spotting the yawners in the crowd—those who are checking their emails

and those who are chatting with their neighbor. *They will all be in your audience.* Practice mentally reassuring yourself—don't let these behaviors shake you or catch you off guard on your big day. Keep a smile on your face as you continue your talk. Again, note the time of the speech to make sure it's in alignment with your slotted time frame. Review the notes to see if you've delivered the main points well.

4. If you're able to do so, deliver round four of your practice speech in the room you'll be delivering your talk while it's empty. Imagine your audience there. If you won't have the opportunity to see the room, see if you can take some photos of the room or even look up where the presentation will take place online; it will take away that "first day of school" syndrome. Concentrate on reviewing the index cards, and give the speech one last time with the index cards.

5. As you deliver the speech this time around, have fun! Speak from your heart. Smile. How'd you do on the time? Do you think the audience will be riveted by your message? Go back through your notes. Whatever you missed, you won't on the final delivery.

Now is the time to put those cards away. Leave one card or paper on the podium, just in case. You're now ready to deliver the talk with passion *from your heart*, knowing you're bringing valuable information to the audience.

These five steps make a difference in how you'll come across to your audience. Instead of watching you read from a script, they'll be engaged by your knowledge and enthusiasm of your message, thus significantly increasing your influence and impact.

If you miss something—so what! No one but you is going to know what you omitted. They will remember your message if they perceive you as self-assured, authoritative, trustworthy, authentic, and passionate. Practice helps you achieve that.

Check out public speaking training organizations online. The Dale Carnegie training programs, for example, teach you how to remove the focus from yourself and put it on the audience and your message. This is the foundation of effective communication and public speaking. Dale Carnegie was the developer of famous courses in interpersonal skills, public speaking, and corporate training. His book *How to Win Friends and Influence People*, from 1936, is a bestseller that remains popular even today. Taking his courses at the age of nineteen put me at an advantage in speaking publicly and with clients. I highly recommend his or other like courses to give you the advantage. You don't need any skills to take the course. It's easy breezy, and you'll benefit greatly.

Continued

> *"Speakers who talk about what life has taught them never fail to keep the attention of their listeners."*
>
> —DALE CARNEGIE

If private coaching or formal training isn't in your budget, find alternatives, such as joining your local Toastmasters group. The Toastmasters experience provides opportunities to gain public speaking practice in a safe environment while getting feedback from group members as you learn. Polished, influential communication is too important to your success—get the help you need to excel.

2. LISTEN TO AND WATCH YOURSELF TALK

Record yourself to hear how you sound and see how you carry yourself so you can see how others view you. This exercise is eye-opening. The first time you listen to your audio, you may say, "That doesn't sound like me at all!" Watching yourself on video might give you a similar shock, but observing yourself in action is one of the most effective ways to determine how you can improve in both your presentations and in your everyday conversations.

First, listen to your audiotape without the video. As you listen, consider whether you are projecting your voice with authority or if you sound intimidated or unsure. Is your breathing shallow? The deeper you breathe, the better your voice projects. The oxygen flowing through your body will help you feel calm and confident. An accomplished vocalist practices her breathing with voice exercises so she can continually improve projection and clarity to ensure her audiences can hear and understand her when she's on stage. Similarly, as a speaker, practice deep and even breathing, projecting a pleasant volume and tone for the sake of your audience.

Next, watch and listen to the video. Watch for posture, gestures, mannerisms, facial expressions, and body language. Assess how your body language affects your spoken words. Have someone else listen to the audio and then watch the video and give feedback as well. Most of your conversation will be in person. You can also practice with your coworkers for your tough conversations on how to position a part of your presentation. People generally are willing to help when asked.

3. BE ARTICULATE

Business conversations and presentations require articulate delivery. People may not remember everything you say, but they will walk away with a strong impression of the way you said it. We've all heard educated people use phrases like, "He did good" instead of "He did well," or when we ask someone how they are, hearing the response, "I'm doing good" instead of "I'm well." These may seem like subtle errors, but using improper English causes your credibility to plummet. You may not recognize your own inarticulate language use if you've been using it throughout your life, so ask a mentor or an executive you've befriended to help you identify whether anything you say sounds unprofessional.

4. NAIL YOUR INTRODUCTIONS

Proper introductions are an art form with definite rules. Learning these rules will ensure you are comfortable and flawless in your greetings and introductions so that everyone feels welcomed. Firm handshake, check. Good eye contact, check again. Be ready for a formal greeting such as, "How do you do, Ms. Jones? It's a pleasure to meet you." No one is going to tell you how important nailing down an introduction is for a professional, but this is a perfect opportunity to give others a good impression of you. Putting forth the extra effort to rehearse the names makes everyone feel welcome and it shows you care. For whatever reason, introductions never come naturally for me. I've botched up one too many and have felt the flatness thereafter. Now I run the names through my head before the introduction, if there's time, or I do a quick mental rehearsal if the introduction is on the spot. Here are a few other key rules for an on-the-spot introduction:

- Look at the person you are speaking to first, then turn to the other person as you complete the introduction.

- Start by introducing the higher-ranked executive or client first. "Ms. CEO, may I introduce John Thomas, our new head executive in the graphic arts department."

- Speak clearly—mumbling defeats the purpose of the introduction.

- Use courteous language. "I'd like to introduce . . ." "May I introduce . . ." "I'd like you to meet . . ." are all good options.

- Use preferred names and titles. In more formal situations, or when there's an obvious age difference, use courtesy titles and last names: "Ms. Samson, I'd like you to meet Mr. Jacobs." This gives Ms. Samson the opportunity to invite Mr. Jacobs to use her first name, or not. Even in informal situations or with your peers, you should use first and last names: "Judy, this is Sam Jacobs. Sam, this is Judy Samson." You can use a nickname if you know the person prefers it.

- Practice. Before walking into a room where you know you will have to provide introductions, rehearse the names. Mix the people up in the room visually. Introductions take effort and you're on the spot. *Make it smooth.*

- It's fine to skip last names when introducing your spouse and children, unless they have a different last name than yours.

- Introduce other family members by their full names, unless they request otherwise. It's also a good idea to mention the family relationship: "Uncle Arthur, may I introduce Mark Weston. Mark, this is my great-uncle, Arthur Pearson."

- When introducing someone to a small group, it's practical to name the group members first, primarily to get their attention: "Sara, Kathy, Dan, I'd like to introduce Curtis Tyler. Curtis, I'd like you to meet Sara Rocher, Kathy Henley, and Dan Quinn."

- Start a conversation. Try to find some topic the people you are introducing have in common: "Sam, I think you and Jake share a passion for Italian wine. Jake might enjoy hearing about your wine tour in northern Italy."

5. PRACTICE COURTESY

Never assume it's a good time for a person to have a conversation with you. When you require someone's time, whether it's an office visit or a phone call, always ask if they have a minute first: "Is this a good time for you to chat for a few minutes" or "Can you tell me when we can talk for a few minutes?" You're the one making the call, so you know it's a good time for you, *but you don't know what the other person's agenda is like.* So ask. Doing so shows respect for the other person and their time—client, colleague, or boss. You gain trust and earn respect in return because you took the time to be courteous.

6. PREPARE IN ADVANCE

To whatever degree possible, start your morning with a look ahead to who and what situations you might encounter that day. Be proactive. Be ready to take the lead when and where it is appropriate. Take five minutes to do the research necessary to effect a successful encounter. Taking time to prepare will ensure you put your best foot forward.

When you are going to be meeting someone for the first time, find out what you can about that person before you sit down with them. Google or research them on the Internet (LinkedIn is a good resource). Five minutes of research will better position you for an effective conversation toward reaching your desired outcome.

When meeting with someone you know to some extent, keep in mind their preferred communication style and plan your discussion accordingly. Do they like details or just the bottom line? Do they like to start with small talk or will they prefer that you get right to the point and keep the conversation to a minimum? Effective communication includes matching your message to fit their style, which you can certainly do with preparation.

7. BE KIND AND BE AUTHENTIC— THEY GO HAND IN HAND

Kindness carries you a long way. Be warm and take a genuine interest in other people. When they feel your authenticity, they'll be much more open to you. Dale Carnegie wisely said, "Listen twice as long as you talk." When you want to hear their point of view and are sincerely interested, the other person will feel that and be more receptive. This means asking yourself: Am I communicating in a way that is easy to understand and will help them accept my message? Am I making it easy for them to openly respond to me, whether or not they agree? *You want the person to want to do it.* What's in it for them? If I can't articulate that, what do I need to do to change my delivery so they do?

8. DON'T COMPLAIN . . . BE A PROBLEM SOLVER AND CREATE A VISION

Leaders don't complain. This is something I had to learn. Don't be the one who points out the problems. Be the one who proposes solutions and enthusiastically creates a vision. That's what leaders do. Save the griping for your friends, and even then do so briefly and move on.

9. SAY IT WITH AUTHORITY

Certain people turn every request or suggestion into a question by raising the pitch of their voice at the end of their sentences. For example, if the statement, "Let's have this project done by Friday," sounds like a question rather than a command, the effectiveness of the deadline is lost. The listener doesn't hear authority, and your directive will sound more like a hope than a mandate. Instead, state your request with authority to denote expectation.

10. SPEAK UP

.....

"The most courageous act is still to think for yourself aloud."

–COCO CHANEL

Make a point to speak up and verbally contribute something worthy in every meeting. Be known for your well-thought-out opinions, questions, and suggestions. Try saying one of these responses if you have something to say and haven't been given the time to be heard:

- Before we move on, I would like us to consider this option.

- Here is why I think this is important . . .

- I have something important I'd like to explain.

Respectfully give your full attention to your colleagues without interruption. You are now requesting to be heard. Present your ideas. If they meet resistance, follow up with probing *how* and *why* questions. When met with opposition, don't be afraid to challenge the group to think through their objections.

11. GIVE IT YOUR ALL . . . AND KNOW WHEN TO BOW OUT GRACEFULLY

Enter each meeting with a clear objective of what you want to accomplish and the value you want to create. Craft your points to persuade through reason, not emotion. Be prepared with rationale, the value of your recommendation, and expected pros and cons. During the presentation, pause now and then—and breathe! Become comfortable with periodic silences. Remember the saying, *The one who speaks last, wins*, and the trick of circling your tongue on the roof of your mouth seven times to keep yourself from jumping in while you let your colleagues talk.

Once you've asked your probing questions and addressed all objections, you may still be faced with opposition and your idea shut down. Don't take it personally. You may be in a position of new information, and you may need to see their point of view. Gracefully accept the rejection and, if appropriate, acknowledge that you see their position—tucking that idea away for another project where it might work. You'll be remembered for how you demonstrated grace under fire. That is true power.

COMMUNICATING FOR YOURSELF

Good communicators also know when and how to communicate themselves to the world. Women often assume that others know what we do and want without our having to say it. Guess what—they don't. So speak up! We need to be vocal about our value when necessary. If you're asking for a raise, be able to succinctly articulate how you've benefited the company and what you can do, moving forward. Make a mental list of your most important accomplishments. You may have a new CEO who doesn't know a thing about your years of dedication; strategically articulate your worth. Don't be shy about what you bring to the table or the research you've done or the successes you've had. Tell them why you are the best person for the position if that's what you're striving for.

Managing Confrontation

Everyone wants to feel heard, and most importantly, everyone wants to feel validated. Consider your communication from the receiving end. Make sure when other people are speaking to you that you take time to understand what they're saying. Ask them to clarify where they're coming from: "What I hear you saying is . . ." and repeat what you've heard back to them in your own words. Ask, "Did I get it?" Listen to their answer, pause, and say, "Is there more?" This is what communication is all about—really listening to the other person. Ensuring someone feels understood eases their concerns, melts opposition, and builds trust, making them more open to what you have to say.

So what happens if you're not being heard? What happens when you're being challenged? Confrontation is inevitable, and the differences between the sexes are clearly apparent in the course of conflict, due to our different styles of communication when things get heated. During conflict, men often employ bargaining, logical argument, and aggression to manage the interaction to win. Women tend to focus on understanding each other's feelings and working toward a win-win. This is a monumental difference and can make compromise between the sexes difficult to reach.

As stated in the previous chapter, male communication is a whole other language. We don't always know the motivation behind what men say. We can't read minds, but based on everything we've covered in this book, we know the only person whose behavior we can truly change is our own—which is often all it takes.

The next time you are in a meeting and your colleagues are dismissing you or talking over you, consider whether there's anything you can do to create a shift in attitude or behavior, as we talked about in chapter one. Take a minute. Analyze how you are communicating, what your body language implies, and how the other people in the room might perceive you as a result. Phyllis Mindell tells us to lead with our strength.

Many of us have been hesitant to use powerful language for fear of seeming "pushy" or in the false belief that to be powerful we have to "act like men". However, it is wrong to believe that power and empathy are mutually exclusive or that powerful language is unwomanly. We don't have to act like men to be strong—we can act like strong women. The language that leads to our success at work is not confrontational, arrogant, or belittling. It does not take power away from or exclude others. Instead, it strengthens us and our ability to transform the corporate culture into one of dignity and civility. Language is the tool with which we define ourselves, our colleagues, and our work place. Transform language and we are able to transform them all.

This quote is a testament to how our shifting can shift others! Are you dragging out details that aren't essential to the issue at hand? Are you sitting back and away from the team instead of leaning in to the thick of things? Are you speaking in a clear, articulate manner that is easily heard by all? Based on how you answer these questions, you can adjust your approach and get back in the game.

IT'S SHOWTIME: ONE-LINERS TO CREATE THE RESULTS YOU WANT

Practicing what you're going to say ahead of time builds your confidence. The same idea can be applied to confrontation by creating a set of one-liners for yourself—little scripts you can commit to memory and pull out beforehand to review when the need arises. We have all come up with great responses hours after the confrontation, but by then it's too late. Having some well-practiced one-liners on

Continued

deck will let you think on your feet when you're put into an uncomfortable situation. Here are a few that are used for sticky situations:

For disagreements of all kinds—

1. Your point has merit; can you explain more?
2. I'm curious. Tell me more.
3. Please, can you elaborate?
4. Please help me become comfortable with your view.
5. I hear what you're saying. There has to be a solution to this.
6. That's interesting. (This makes them think about what they're saying.)

If there's something you don't agree with and you don't want to answer right away—

1. Let me give it some thought.
2. Thank you for your input. Let me take some time to process it, and I'll get back to you.
3. Let's agree to disagree at this point and reconvene later to talk further.
4. Our perspectives on this are different. Let's bookmark this and reconvene when we've had time to sit with it a bit. Is tomorrow (setting some date is respectful) good for you?

These options give both parties an opportunity to think things over, calm down if necessary, and meet again at a time that works for both schedules. Use the twenty-four-hour rule to cool down. *Never tell someone they're wrong*; often conflict comes down to perspective. You may both be right. You may both be wrong. There's *always* three sides to the story—yours, mine, and reality. Getting back to the issue later gives you space to realize this.

When someone responds to you in a negative way—

1. Okay.
2. Thanks for sharing that.
3. The data doesn't compute. Let's go back and check on this.

This eliminates their defensiveness by releasing the rope before any tug-of-war starts. Much more can be accomplished when the energy is focused on the real issue at hand. This was a battle my husband, Jerry, and I had when he became my full-time partner. Once we dropped the ropes in the tug-of-war over whose method was better, we accomplished ten times more. The last answer here also allows you to defuse an argument and work together to find out where the train derailed. You're not saying they're wrong, but you're not saying you're wrong either. You're acknowledging your perceptions are different.

When someone confronts you, yells, or raises their voice—

1. This issue needs further discussion so it can be resolved. Let's do so in a professional and respectful manner we're both capable of.

Continued

2. Why don't we take a breather here? Let's bookmark this and come back when we both have cooled off.

3. Hmm. Why don't we start this conversation over.

4. This conversation is getting uncomfortable. Let's revisit it later.

5. That's not how I'm seeing things.

6. That doesn't deserve to be commented on. Let's reconvene tomorrow.

7. Avoid making a scene. Even if the other person is upset, don't react. Think, then act. When you are cornered and someone confronts you, speak in a way that diffuses the situation. Plus, *when you remain calm, others realize quickly who's out of control and who's not.*

When you want to express an opinion that may not be popular—

1. This is something I believe in.

2. I am speaking from years of experience.

3. Please allow me to be frank here.

4. There's something I need to get off my chest; do you have a moment? If not, when is a good time for you?

These statements express an opinion. They cannot be agreed or disagreed with because you're simply stating your opinion, just as they are.

If you have to bring something negative to someone's attention—

1. There is something you should know.
2. I don't take lightly what I am about to say.
3. There is no other way I know to tell you this.
4. It may be uncomfortable for you to hear this, and I'm uncomfortable saying it.

If someone is nit-picking with you or belaboring a point out of context—

1. Is there a reason why you're so invested in this?

You're calling them on their point.

When you're firm about something and a subordinate is challenging you—

1. It's my decision. It's not up for discussion.

Effective communication is a two-way street. If someone doesn't agree with you, don't assume you understand, because sometimes our assumptions are wrong. But also don't be afraid to ask *why*. This is especially important when communicating with men. If they think something is important and they disagree with your view, ask them why with open-ended questions. Encourage them to share their views as opposed to responding with a yes or no. We want to encourage the other person to share a differing opinion with us. We should address it, and it just might be a really good idea.

.....

"Don't think of knocking out another person's brains because he differs in opinion from you. It'd be just as rational to knock yourself on the head because you differ from yourself ten years ago."

–HORACE MANN

How to Handle Inappropriate Behavior

When someone raises their voice, becomes offensive, or acts aggressively toward you in a meeting, the best thing to do *at that moment* is nothing. Don't engage. Instead, in a calm voice, say okay and know you will address it later. The more frustrated they become, the louder they can become. Aggressive personalities often raise their voices in a last ditch effort when they know they're wrong and feel they may "lose"—don't bite. Keep your calm demeanor.

Instead, address inappropriate behavior after the meeting in private. Go to them and say, "I'd like to have a few minutes of your time." If they're busy, then say, "When can we meet because we need to talk—today." Give them a small time frame to address it. Doing so expeditiously shows them that you won't be walked all over. Taking the high road and address-ing negative behavior privately is respectful—and it's what we would want someone to do for us.

My friend Sue Maniloff gives the perfect example of taking the high road:

"As a director representing an industry-leading global orga-nization, I was attending a large international conference in order to network, develop business, and attend informational sessions on different aspects of the industry. There were sev-eral people from diverse areas of my organization who were also in attendance, all staying at the same hotel.

"Breakfast was provided for us each morning, with open seating among our group. I saw two men who I have known professionally for years sitting together. These men were both senior executives in the organization, on the leadership team, and in their upper forties. They were working together on a project I was also involved with. I had provided them with some critical, supportive information. As I approached their table, I asked if their conversation was a confidential one or if I could join them for a quick breakfast before our long day ahead at the conference. They both looked at each other and then looked at me and said, 'No reason for you to sit here. We are talking about all of the attractive women that are here at this conference. We're not discussing business.' I was actu-ally shocked. It was 2012 and not 1958! I quickly responded, 'Since I am here to discuss business, I'll find another seat!' It's like the old Fred Astaire and Ginger Rogers story: Women do everything that men do, only backward and in high heels! My own modern-day workplace interpretation of that line is to always be at the top of your game, be fully prepared, keep it professional, and never let them see you sweat. This is the best way I've handled confrontation in the workplace over the years. Of course, that strategy has typically led me to outperform confrontational men, which has on occasion positioned me as a threat. That is yet another story . . ."

Unfortunately, we cannot talk about communication and confrontation without addressing the issue of sexual harassment. If someone is harassing you sexually or being verbally abusive to you, they are in the wrong. Period. If someone asks you out and you're not interested, say, "No, thank you." If they ask you again, say, "I believe you have asked me before. The answer is still the same. No, thank you." If it happens a third time, well, three strikes and you're out. Firmly say, "This has to stop." Turn around, walk away, and report the harassment to management, if you work in a quality environment, or if not, to human resources.

If you are being womanized, speak to your superiors. If you are being harassed, the other person's behavior is intolerable, illegal, and it's up to the firm to handle it. No one should tolerate being harassed, man or woman. When human resources asks how you handled it, answer honestly and without culpability.

Managing Unrealistic Expectations

You're probably wondering why the topic of managing unrealistic expectations would be included in a chapter about communication. Too often, women are prone to not want to disappoint. We say yes when we should be saying no. We would rather not admit we are biting off more than we can chew. It's important to be prepared on what to say before the situation arises instead of taking a project on that won't be a true reflection of your work.

What do you do when someone asks you to do something that's unrealistic, like asking for something to be done by five when it's already three thirty and the task will take several hours? Assuming this isn't a business emergency and it's more of a repeat performance of the colleague or a superior, state, "This is a five-hour job that requires more time than the two hours available to do this project effectively and professionally. How do you propose we manage this?" Then give them some options for now and moving forward. This states your situation in a rational and unemotional way and tells the person what you need to meet their expectation.

If you have too much on your plate, say enthusiastically, "This is what I'm working on and the deadlines I have for each project. Please tell me how you would like me to prioritize what I have here." This is helpful in making the other person aware of what you have on your plate, and it also makes them responsible for what does get accomplished. It sets realistic expectations and shows you're working as a team player.

If It's Time to Fold

We can always learn to handle situations differently; there's always something we can do to improve. At the same time, you have to realize when enough is enough. If you have shifted your communication approach and you're still not getting results and not getting ahead, and you've talked to a mentor about it and are still experiencing communication problems at work, you've reached a point when you have to consider that the situation may not be a good fit. Only you know when it's time to look for other opportunities where you will be happier, valued, and validated. No professional should have to accept poor treatment to get ahead.

You may be in a group of people who are not emotionally healthy—there's always a few—but if 70 percent of your company is dysfunctional, it's time to move on! Do what you can to improve your communications and rely on feedback. Make a decision. Listen to your gut. It is important to be true to yourself and understand your circumstances. Further, don't feel like you must prove yourself repeatedly to those who don't care or care to change. *You are responsible for your own welfare.*

A friend of mine who is a former vice president at a Fortune 100 technology company knows this truth well. Her story illustrates key principles of communication, as well as a deep understanding of her own professional needs.

"I owned a small publishing company. A client and good friend of mine recruited me to be vice president of education at the company where he was a vice president. The company was in crisis and a new CEO was recruited from one of the top six consulting companies. The CEO was well known for demeaning all of the women in the company. Following a weekend training event for the new executive team, the CEO turned to the group and said, 'Would you all agree with me that Ellen here contributed more than anyone else to the success of the weekend? To acknowledge her efforts, I have written her a very nice check. Nice going, Ellen.'

"I was personally and professionally humiliated. It was mid-December. I went to my office and wrote a note to the CEO, thanking him for his gesture, but pointing out that, 'At this time of the year, when many families struggle to buy gifts for their children, I would ask that the enclosed check I am returning to you be donated to Toys for Tots or another charity in the spirit of the season.' I never heard a word from the CEO, but in the end, he embarrassed me yet again. On Valentine's Day, another female vice president stopped by my office and asked, 'Did you get yours yet?' When I said no, she said, 'Hold on to your chair. Wally has used the money you returned to him to buy a single rose for every female employee in the company for Valentine's Day.' I received my rose, packed up my office, and resigned from the company."

Sometimes, resigning is the only option, and while it may seem counterintuitive, it can be the best professional step we can take if it means we no longer have to submit ourselves to a toxic work environment. When you close a door behind you, it forces you to open the door ahead of you, often with better opportunities you wouldn't have otherwise known about.

Verbal Communication and Your Success

We know that today there are more women than men in graduate school. There are more women than men in medical school. Men and women have miscommunicated for long enough. We can make communication and conflict a win-win by being strong women, taking the first step, and showing men how to adjust their communication to include us.

Our goal is to help men understand, and we must be willing to teach them how to work with us. If you have good rapport with your male colleagues, let them know they can and should ask you for your input and include you in the decision-making process if they're not currently including you. If both sexes work together, we win together, and that is the ultimate goal.

As women, by adjusting our communication approach to all genders, we will gain confidence as well as earn trust and respect we so desperately want. Let's empower ourselves to go after those higher positions with vigor and, in turn, achieve equal pay.

What Is No One Telling You?

THINGS TO REMEMBER . . .

- Establish a communication avatar and mentally consult with them when perplexed. Think about how they would successfully handle things.

- Nail down your introductions. Leaders are flawless at introductions.

- Practice important presentations five times.

- Condition yourself to become comfortable being challenged. Be prepared. Dissolve all defensiveness. It's just business.

- Keep communication responses in your notes on your phone or computer. Review before tough meetings until they become second nature.

PLAN OF ACTION

As a result of what I learned in chapter 5, I am going to

Stop doing—

- _____

- _____

Start doing–

- _____

- _____

Continue doing–

- _____

- _____

Chapter Six

create space: body language skills you need to know

.....

"Language is a more recent technology. Your body language, your eyes, your energy will come through to your audience before you even start speaking."

—PETER GUBER

Did you know something as small as where your hands are placed in a meeting can affect how other people feel about you? What you have to say is not the only way you influence others' decisions. Verbal communication is only one piece of the puzzle. What we say without words is equally critical. In this chapter, I hope to emphasize the importance of body language and how it can help you read others and position yourself for success.

Some years ago, my company offered employees an opportunity to participate in a training program that taught us how to use body language to help build trust with clients. This was my first lesson in body language, and I was surprised to learn how powerful a role it plays. Did you know that when you're in a meeting or any business dealing with a client, keeping your hands on top of the table helps reassure the clients that you aren't hiding anything? And when you're sitting across from someone, keeping two feet on the floor and facing the person directly expresses that you're equal? These aren't gestures most of us would consciously note during an interaction, but they absolutely play a role in the three seconds it takes a person to make a decision about you. Mastering body language provides a whole new set of communication skills you can use to effect a positive outcome in important business negotiations.

According to Susanne Jones, associate professor of communication studies at the University of Minnesota, 65–75 percent of all communication is nonverbal in nature. As she puts it, nonverbal cues give us information "to make sense of how we feel and think about others. People use nonverbal cues to arrive at judgments about how they relate to coworkers or to interpret employee performance."[18] Body language reveals your feelings and meanings to others *and* reveals their feelings and meanings

---

18 Leslie Contreras Schwartz, "Nonverbal Communication with Workplace Interactions," *Chron*, accessed December 14, 2016, http://smallbusiness.chron.com/nonverbal-communication-workplace-interactions-844.html.

to you. This exchange of information happens on conscious and unconscious levels. Body language can't be hidden.

When a person's nonverbal communication contradicts their verbal communication, your subconscious notices it in a matter of seconds. If someone's forehead shows perspiration and they are avoiding eye contact while trying to convince you of something, you know in your gut that something is wrong. If a colleague tries to console you by saying, "Oh, I'm so sorry for your loss" while checking her text messages, you won't feel as if that person is the least bit genuine. Build trust by keeping your verbal and nonverbal messages aligned.

Reading body language is not something that's taught in schools. Some executives never even pay attention to the value it could bring to their career. It is an unspoken method of communication that is hugely important: It makes for happy clients and clearer understanding in any business negotiation. Not only will it be beneficial to you in reading people but will also help you in delivering the right message.

Karen Beisch, vice president of human resources for a portfolio of diverse companies, shared the following story, illustrating how she communicated successfully:

"When I was twenty-four years old, I found myself at the beginning of my career in human resources. I was a young, degreed, independent young woman ready to work hard and tackle problems in the automotive industry. At the time,

Continued

I was the only female manager in a predominantly male environment. Not having a mentor, I found that, to make a point, I would mimic the aggressive behavior of my male counterparts. When they raised their voice in a meeting, I did as well. When they used rough language, I felt that I needed to do the same on occasion to be heard. I would ignore my intuition and use only information that was fact based because I felt that intuition would not sell the point I was making. Essentially, I tried to go toe-to-toe with my male counterparts using their behavior to show that I was serious and I could keep up. I would come home at night exhausted and unhappy.

"A few years later, when I was more secure with my career, I looked back and realized that I couldn't win using this approach. It was their approach, not mine, and it did not fit for me as a woman. Being strong but also feminine does not equate to weakness in the work world. I realized that while many intelligent women can have the facts and be very prepared for meetings with data in hand, we have the gift of intuition and this is a gift that women must cherish and cultivate, rather than ignore. Intuition, combined with facts and preparedness, gives us an advantage in accomplishing our goals. As I reflected, I realized that in situations where I did not make the best decisions, I had ignored my intuition, which had been correct. My best decisions come forth when I use all of the tools available, including data and intuition. To this day, I consider and draw upon both, regardless of the environment. This was a difficult but significant lesson to learn, and I am thankful for the experience. The lessons you learn the hard way are the very lessons you don't forget!"

Where the "Feminine" Advantage Falls Short

Women tend to have the advantage when it comes to body language. We naturally use our body language to express affinity and intimacy in order to bond with people and let them know we're listening. We smile more and are better at keeping eye contact than men. We stand closer to others. We lean forward rather than back in a chair while listening, and we face a person directly rather than turning to one side. We touch and use gestures that indicate a desire to reach out to the other person. We use this body language to establish connections. We're also better at reading body language because we're so intuitive.

However, women, particularly in business environments, fall short when it comes to using body language to communicate power and confidence. Research shows that people who can see and those who are blind from birth both raise their hands to celebrate athletic victory. Keeping your voice tone low (not high pitched or raised); not forcing a smile as you are speaking (it looks insincere); keeping eye contact with whom you are speaking with; not crossing your legs, especially when standing; keeping your palms open; not raising your arms or crossing your arms; and not talking with your hands are just some of the ways to maintain a more universally powerful appearance. Try talking with your hands on your hips. This body language will allow men to look at you as more of an equal, and it will give you confidence.

Understanding and implementing the nonverbal indicators of confidence and power will drastically affect your workplace behavior and put you on par with the men who understand these indicators intuitively.

In *Gender and the Body Language of Power*, Lisa Wade, PhD, professor at Occidental College, writes that philosopher Sandra Lee Bartky once observed that being feminine often means using one's body to portray powerlessness. Research has shown that expansive body postures that take up room instill a psychological sense of power and entitlement. The fact that this behavior is gendered may help explain the persistence of gender inequality and, more pointedly, some men's belief that they have earned their unearned privileges. As women, we move and situate our bodies in ways that take up less space. We take smaller steps, for example. Men spread out more, gesture more freely, and carry themselves in a more relaxed manner. Men often perceive the person with the more relaxed posture as having higher status. Women are said to have smaller personal space bubbles. These behaviors reinforce gender stereotypes of male independence and assertiveness and female dependency and passivity.

THE 10 COMMANDMENTS OF COMMUNICATION:

1. I shall match the tone of my voice and my body language with the message I want to communicate.
2. I shall be honest, open, and willing to hear the other points of view with enthusiasm.
3. When it's showtime, I shall shift the attention and nervousness away from myself and concentrate on the message I want my audience to receive.
4. I shall rehearse my talking points or conversation with the end result in mind, at least once for a one-on-one and five times for a larger audience.
5. I shall summarize at the end of my presentation with a plan of action and explain the rationale.
6. I shall be authentic in my delivery, be willing to tackle tough questions with sincerity, and handle frivolous questions by asking them to meet afterward or to hold the question until the end of the presentation.
7. I shall remember I was given two ears and one mouth for a reason and to take the time to listen and validate the other person's point of view, whether or not I agree and without judgment.
8. I shall deliver negative news with facts and honesty about a situation and an expectation of communicating future information as it becomes available.
9. I shall know my audience and adjust my content and delivery accordingly. I shall be cognizant my delivery isn't condescending to my audience.
10. I shall deliver my message with clarity of facts, not opinions, unless asked. I shall keep my message simple and easy to understand.

Presence is a combination of having confidence, passion, and enthusiasm and being captivating, authentic, and comfortable. You've heard the saying, "Fake it until you make it." We can dress the part and talk the talk, whether we feel confident and powerful or not. And when it comes to confidence, faking it can actually make a person feel more confident.

In her highly viewed TED Talk discussion "Your Body Language Shapes Who You Are" Amy Cuddy, a social psychologist from Harvard, discusses the science behind this phenomenon. Studies show that our body language—and the confidence we project—affects how people see us. Additionally, adopting power poses changes our body chemistry. Confident leaders have low levels of cortisol (the hormone that counteracts stress) and high levels of testosterone. Cuddy's research also shows that adopting power poses lowers your cortisol and increases testosterone, instantly making you feel more confident than you did moments before. Her studies reveal that people who practice a high-power pose for five minutes before a critical evaluation showed lower cortisol and fewer outward signs of stress, such as an anxious smile or biting your lip. Further, people who expand and use confident body postures during job interviews are more likely to get hired for jobs than those who sit slumped or with their body folding forward. Amy's book *Presence: Bringing Your Boldest Self to Your Biggest Challenges* is a great read for every executive.

Learning and practicing body language skills is a huge benefit for women in both their business and personal lives. By controlling our posture, we elevate how we carry ourselves; doing so makes us feel and project confidence. As Cuddy explained it, "Our bodies change our minds and our minds change our behavior and our behavior changes our outcomes."

Amy's study of interviewees was separated into two groups. The first group went into the interview without any instruction. The second group was taught power poses before they entered the interview room. The applicants in the second group *nailed* the interviews.

How do you carry yourself? Do you know? Are you aware of what you are projecting to those around you?

Tip 1: Stand in front of a full-length mirror in your natural stance. Watch the change as you stand tall, raise your head high, and pull your shoulders back. You can see the changes as your body adjusts, triggering confidence in your mind. In any given situation, you will feel more confident and be perceived as more optimistic, risk-averse, and capable. Portraying confidence through body language gives you the presence you desire.

Tip 2: Feeling a bit nervous? Try this exercise: For a confidence booster, imagine standing ten times taller than whomever you're speaking with. Be big in your mind. Speak with authority. It will affect your persona magically.

Harness Your Inner Power

To be successful at power poses, start by being conscious of how your body is positioned. Make a cognizant effort to straighten your posture and expand your chest. Don't shrink—hold your head high. Capture your share of body space.

Anytime you're about to enter a situation where you'll be evaluated, such as in a job interview, when asking for a promotion, or when giving a presentation, take a few minutes to go to a restroom mirror and adopt the Wonder Woman pose: Stand in front of a mirror with your hands on your hips and your chest held high. See if you don't walk into the meeting with more confidence.

Once you master your own body language, start watching other people's body language as a way to gather information. The ability to look around a room and gauge what's happening based on each person's body language will give you a huge advantage in any given situation. Who is confident or unsure or doesn't know what they're talking about? This information is power.

Body language helps determine if your message is being heard. Let's say you're in a room, whether with a client or business colleague, and you notice they're folding their arms. This should tell you that they have questions, feel defensive, or are not engaged for some reason. Their body language is closed. Being able to read their body language gives you the opportunity to find out what the roadblock is by addressing it then and there. Ask probative questions to open up your audience and get them talking. You likely won't get another chance. Addressing defensive body language allows you to serve the true needs of clients more than your competition, and it will likely create an upturn in your business because they trust that you have their best interests at heart.

Mirroring: The Other Way We Communicate

Mirroring is when a person subconsciously imitates the gesture, speech pattern, or attitude of another. It is the subconscious replication of another person's nonverbal signals. This occurs in everyday interactions and often goes unnoticed by both the person enacting the mirroring behaviors as well as the individual who is being mirrored.

When you want to connect with someone and build trust, mirroring their body language is an effective approach. For example, when they put their hands on their hips, you can move your hands to your hips to mirror them, thereby subconsciously conveying connection, friendliness, and openness. A small gesture can unconsciously establish a powerful connection and rapport. The similarities in nonverbal gestures allow each party to feel more connected and to therefore believe that they share similar attitudes and ideas. It promotes a sense of engagement and belonging within the situation. It's the connection of "like to like." This is something executives aren't conscious of, and knowing this Unspoken Code will help you establish a level playing field.

Once during a problem-solving meeting with four men, I began to sense that my ideas weren't being heard or seriously considered. The body language of one gentleman in particular, who was sitting with his hands in a steeple on the table in front of him, indicated to me that he didn't want to hear my opinion. Holding one's hands in this way is considered a power position. Looking across the table, I saw that another gentleman was doing this as well. I needed the chance to make my point, but they were sending the message they didn't want to hear it. I mirrored them and put my hands in a steeple position to let them know I was holding my ground. Honestly, I wasn't comfortable holding my hands like that. Once I matched the steeple, one of the gentlemen started moving his steeple up and down. So I did the same. By this time, it took everything in me to keep from laughing. They never noticed the mirroring. It worked, and they backed down and began to engage with me.

Rebekah Campbell, tech entrepreneur and founder of posse.com, shares a similar strategy for building confidence through body language on her Posse Blog. Before presenting her business to investors and other individuals from the finance industry, she'd visit the nearest restroom and stand in front of the mirror in a victory pose, with her hands above her head in a V position, for at least two minutes. This would remind her to take up as much space as possible during meetings, which in turn led to her feeling confident and assertive.

As she notes, "This is the opposite of my natural instincts, but it worked!" Whether you're at home, at work, or in a social situation, be mindful of what people are communicating—verbally and nonverbally. Mirroring body language is a powerful strategy you can use to increase a person's receptiveness to your ideas and recommendations.[19]

Letting Go of Tension

Women hold stress differently than men. We often bottle our stress up until pressure builds up and the cork wants to shoot off. But, as author and speaker Joyce Meyer says, "When you bury something alive, it stays alive." Once bottled up, these feelings won't go away unless they are addressed somehow, somewhere. Men don't allow their focus to be diluted with personal issues nearly as much as women do. Note to self: *Stay focused.* Don't worry about what your partner said last night or whether or not your children are happy and on the right road or how you feel about what the last month's holiday treats have done to your waistline. We need to set all the little things aside so we don't let them increase our stress. When our worries are weighing on us, it shows.

One day, just before a presentation, I stepped down the

---

19 Rebekah Campbell, "The Unexpected Impact of Changing My Body Language," *Posse Blog*, September 24, 2014, http://www.rebekahcampbell.com/2014/09/25/the-unexpected-impact-of-changing-my-body-language/.

hall to the restroom. As I was washing my hands, I saw my reflection in the mirror. It was scary. I thought, "Oh, my God! This woman is a walking stress time bomb." I looked *so* tense. (I can't even remember why.) It was a wake-up call. I quickly stretched my eyes, mouth, neck, shoulders, and arms. Good thing the restroom was empty, because I'm sure I looked silly.

No one wants to listen to someone who's tense. The audience will become as tense as the speaker. We want to listen to people who are confident and relaxed. We may not be excited about or looking forward to every presentation, interview, or meeting due to the personal space we are in, but we need to look as though we are. Be sure and stretch your face, neck, and shoulders and take a few deep breaths before meetings to make sure you align your attitude and physical presence. Do a quick mirror check if there's one available. You can even take a quick selfie. Does your face show you are happy to be there and excited about what you have to share? Are your shoulders straight and your posture energetic? Does your face and body language radiate with the message you want your audience or client to receive? Try it. You'll perform better and exude a confidence that will inspire others to have confidence in you too.

Body Language and Success

We are human and we are connected, even when we stand on different sides of the table. Our most basic life goals are the same. We all want to be happy in our lives and successful in our work, and we want to leave something behind that we can be proud of. These deep human desires are often expressed in the way we carry ourselves.

Learn to use body language effectively. The more you practice, the more natural it will become. Use it as a means toward understanding. Read the body language signals to see what people need so you can meet those needs successfully. Studies tell us many women could use a confidence booster from time to time. By putting these tried and true body language techniques to use, you will command positive attention from your business interactions and increase your confidence in any setting, business or otherwise.

Get to it, Wonder Woman!

What Is No One Telling You?

THINGS TO REMEMBER . . .

- Nonverbal language makes up the majority of communication. Become an expert in reading these skills to interpret and deliver messages.

- Take up space! Mirror how businessmen in your discussions hold court.

- If in doubt, remember: Keep direct eye contact and equal weight in your feet. Keep your palms open or on top of the table. Use steeple hands when challenged to show you count as much as they do. And remember your Wonder Woman stance!

- Do a self-check on your own body language. Relaxed? Breathing deeply to show you are in control?

PLAN OF ACTION

As a result of what I learned in chapter 6, I am going to

Stop doing–

- _____

- _____

Start doing–

- _____

- _____

Continue doing–

- _____

- _____

PART THREE

Dress
the
Part

Chapter Seven

the importance of dressing for success

.....

"The first impression is a lasting impression . . .
violate protocol, express yourself as you will, but be
aware that others will make life-altering decisions
about you, of which you may forever be unaware."

–JOHN BANDLER

Having been raised in the funeral business, I was taught to dress well for certain occasions. If a family was coming in to make arrangements, my parents dressed up for the occasion. But when I was a single mom, I didn't start out with much of a wardrobe. I became friends with a man named Roger, one of the owners of a fine-dining establishment I worked at after I left my abusive relationship. He heard about my circumstances and, as an attorney, his firm helped me pro bono with my divorce. I was so appreciative someone was kind enough to throw me a line, and we stayed in touch.

After hearing I had taken the job at E. F. Hutton, Roger called me up one day and invited me out to meet a friend of his, who was a local celebrity author and psychologist, for lunch. I was a bit nervous, not having the best wardrobe, and asked Roger what I should wear. Roger said, "You know that conservative tweed suit you wore during your last visit in our office? I would wear that." I would have never guessed that "boring" suit would have been the thing to wear to this luncheon. But I pulled it out from the back of my closet and wore it to lunch with his friend. I looked around the restaurant and noticed that I blended right in with the rest of the business-people around me. This gave me the confidence to act like I was one of them. Despite feeling tremendously out of place, the image I was presenting was a manifestation of the path toward the powerful businesswoman I yearned to become. As Roger and his friend engaged in witty conversation and I did my best to chime in, I happily acknowledged to myself that nobody there but me could know that I had only a dollar in my wallet until my next paycheck.

My positive attitude and open communication helped me make a lasting impression. But my carefully chosen outfit was the icing on the cake. Not only did it allow me to feel confident, it indicated to those in my midst that I was there to be taken seriously. I didn't know it at the time, but Roger had given me crucial insight into the Unspoken Code of business:

Nobody wants to say it, but appearances *do* matter. In fact, they can make or break your professional career.

Even though you may not put weight on how you dress, and feel you shouldn't be judged any differently than men, it's the simple truth that your appearance sends a message. I'll be blunt: If a woman wears a form-fitting blouse, she will be stared at by male colleagues. Pretending the male gaze doesn't exist is a waste of time and energy. When closely involved with the opposite sex, you have to keep a standard of professional dress that minimizes the possibility of distraction. My advice: Make things easy on yourself and take this out of the equation. In our previous sections, we have outlined the ways we can lay down the foundation for a successful career and the ways we can begin to project that success from the inside out. In this last portion of the book, I want to give you the tools to solidify that image of success by telling you exactly how you can look the part of professional businesswoman. But before we get to the *hows* in the next chapter, let's dive into the *whys*. Why, in this day and age, should we care about how we look?

The Three-Second Impression

As an illustration, say you are about to board a plane. As you pass the cockpit, you look inside. You see the pilot sporting a five-day-old beard and a crumpled tee shirt. Would you feel comfortable getting on a plane this man is flying? What if your new doctor were to enter the exam room dressed in cutoff jeans, flip flops, and sporting dirty hair under a baseball cap? How relaxed would you feel sitting there in your thin paper gown ready for an exam? We don't consciously judge people based on their appearance. We've been told it's wrong to judge a book by its cover, but we have definite expectations about what a professional—*any professional*—should look like. Here's why.

It's called the amygdala hijack, a term coined by Dr. Daniel Goleman in his 1996 book *Emotional Intelligence: Why It Can Matter More Than IQ* and drawn from the work of Joseph E. LeDoux. Goleman used the term to describe emotional responses from people that are immediate and overwhelming and out of measure with the actual stimulus because they trigger a much more significant emotional threat. Goleman states, "All emotions are, in essence, impulses to act, the instant plans for handling life that evolution has instilled in us."

It goes back to our primitive days on how our brain works to protect us. Think caveman or cavewoman and the saber-toothed tiger. Your brain screams, "Danger!" The blood flows from your brain to your extremities to help you. Does the cavewoman need to fight the tiger or flee from the tiger?

This is why those few seconds are so important when you meet someone new. The human brain quickly sizes up the people we encounter. When someone walks into the room, the primitive area in our brain (the amygdala) that's responsible for our fight or flight decision-making process reacts. Within three seconds, it makes a judgment based on the person's physical appearance, what they are wearing, and their mannerisms. Is she friend or foe? Is she trustworthy?

So think about this: While you are judging others, they are also judging you. Your appearance is the first thing people see, and it speaks volumes. Before you say a single word, others form an impression of who you are based on your attire and grooming—from your hair down to your shoes. Based on this amygdala hijack, they decide whether or not you can be trusted. In her book *You've Only Got Three Seconds*, Camille Lavington writes, "These appraisals are being made constantly, in both business and social life. You've hardly said a word, but once this three-second evaluation is over, the content of your presentation can't change it."

It is said that some people who are educated in this area can recognize the rapid response of the hijack or have a deep mindfulness about it and can possibly overcome it. Why take the chance? Don't bank on it. Make that first impression count.

Camille further states, "People who are open to modifying these attributes have ego strength: so much confidence in what's underneath that they don't find it threatening to contemplate adjusting their manners or clothing to make others feel more comfortable . . . Business and social life are the stage, and we are the actors. Costume is just a tool we use to help create the illusion. I'm not telling you to run out and blow your savings on a designer wardrobe. I'm telling you to dress the part, whatever that requires."

The bottom line is to step it up: Be polished and fit the part. It's not about losing your authenticity. It's about being the best *you* possible.

Building a good first impression as a business professional is imperative. Whatever your field, relationships are job one. It's about trust. You put your trust in a professional to provide the help you seek. When you hire an attorney, you trust them to represent you well in the courtroom. You trust that your CPA is knowledgeable and honest. In any business transaction, you must feel confident that the analysis has been done well and in your best interest. You're not going to feel that trust if the person is dressed like they just rolled out of bed, is heading for the beach, or in some other way is obviously not putting their best foot forward.

I'm not saying this is fair or just: We should be able to appeal to our more evolved natures and overcome these snap judgments. In nonbusiness settings, we are aware of this and are often able to do just that. But the business world is different. Snap judgments count, and what is expected goes unspoken. What makes people able and willing to trust others in business also goes unspoken. But trust isn't only a feeling people have or not: Trust can be cultivated by a number of nonverbal cues, and you should put every effort into understanding what those cues are.

To be successful in your chosen profession, it's critical to fulfill the expectations of your clients and potential clients when they think about a person in your line of work. *Your appearance is part of their holistic experience in working with you and the company you represent.* It's in your best interest to make this holistic experience happen.

This isn't to suggest you put on an act or not be yourself. Simply put: If you want your internal qualities to shine through and be recognized, start by dressing the part of those in the top of your field. This, inarguably, is twice as critical to women in male-dominated fields such as finance, law, accounting, investment banking, medicine, psychiatry, insurance, information technology, automotive, and so on. By taking conscious control of your appearance, you are giving yourself every opportunity to make those first three seconds a success—and setting yourself up to make a lasting impression that extends far beyond these first moments. What is there to lose?

Dress Well to Be More Effective

Not only does dressing intentionally benefit how you come across in that three-second impression, it increases the quality of work you do as well. Researchers at Northwestern University Kellogg School of Management found that when research subjects wore a uniform, such as a lab coat, their attention spans increased during specific tasks.[20] This

---

20 Sandra Blakeslee, "Mind Games: Sometimes a White Coat Isn't Just a White Coat," *The New York Times*, April 2, 2012, http://www.nytimes.com/2012/04/03/science/clothes-and-self-perception.html?emc=eta1.

strongly suggests that dressing professionally will help you become a better professional. When people dress to impress for work, they work more effectively and are more focused. You feel confident when you look your best. If you feel you've underdressed or are fearful of a wardrobe malfunction, you can't concentrate as well on the task, discussion, or presentation at hand.

Dr. Karen Pine, fashion psychologist and professor of psychology at the University of Hertfordshire in England, suggests that dressing casually could cause an employee to feel less focused and alert. "When we put on an item of clothing, it is common for the wearer to adopt the characteristics associated with that garment. A lot of clothing has symbolic meaning for us, whether it's 'professional work attire' or 'relaxing weekend wear,' so when we put it on we prime the brain to behave in ways consistent with that meaning."

The research from Dr. Karen Pine, and other clothing research described in her book *Mind What You Wear: The Psychology of Fashion*, shows how people's mental processes and perceptions can be primed by clothing. Professor Pine describes how women who were given a math test performed worse when wearing a swimsuit than when wearing a sweater and how putting on a white coat improved people's mental agility because their brain was primed to take on the mental capacities they associated with being a doctor.

When your outward appearance complements your vocation, talents, and contributions, you can feel assured that your client, boss, or coworker will be more attentive to your brilliant ideas. Before you're ready to walk out the door, look at yourself in the mirror. Do you look the part? What do people see when they look at you? Be honest with yourself. Is your appearance promoting you or holding you back?

My friend Susan Perlin has the following to say about the link between what we wear and how effective we can be:

"Many of the meetings I attend (internal firm management meetings, client or board meetings, and new client proposal meetings) are with mostly men. I choose my clothes carefully, depending on whom I will be interacting with throughout the day. My good friend and fellow female partner at my firm teases me about my 'power look.' She can always tell when I have an important meeting. I believe you can gain instant, easy credibility by dressing for power. For me (and my industry, public accounting), this means a good fitting (not too tight, not too short), current, conservative suit, conservative shoes, and conservative jewelry. You can lose credibility instantly by not dressing appropriately. I am at my best and most confident if I feel confident with what I'm wearing and if I'm totally prepared for the meeting."

Fighting Gender Stereotypes

Dressing well doesn't only do us a service to ourselves; it does a service to all working women by slowly chipping away at the gender stereotypes that have been drummed into you by film and print advertising throughout your life. Magazines and television have told us that you should look beautiful and sexy. Media stylists and costume designers are particularly aware of the messages that can be telegraphed through a carefully considered sexist wardrobe. Show some skin. Flaunt your assets. When you do, you get attention. Men look at you. Women look at you. People notice, but they're not noticing what really matters. By dressing professionally and classy, you put sexist and objectifying ideas of how a woman should dress to rest.

These sexist messages are everywhere. In recent years, the push to look sexy has infiltrated weekly TV episodes and even the news. Female newscasters are delivering vital information to the public dressed in too-tight or too-short dresses, thick and heavy false eyelashes, hair extensions, and five-inch heels. They get attention, for sure. Unfortunately, these women do not send the impression of an accomplished, intelligent professional woman. Instead, dressing this way only serves to reiterate the stereotype that women should be prized for our beauty and sexuality rather than for our intellectual abilities.

Anne Doyle, my friend and author of *Powering Up! How America's Women Achievers Become Leaders*, spoke candidly with me about media channels, especially Fox News. "Women of every age and every level of professional achievement are continuously judged by their appearance, while men can have wild hair, disheveled clothing, and be seriously overweight and still command respect, which would never be given to women whose appearance was similar."

To prove this point, anchorman Karl Stefanovic from Australia wore the same suit every day for a year. Guess what? No one noticed! After the experiment, Karl commented, "I'm judged on my interviews, my appalling sense of humor—on how I do my job, basically. Whereas women are quite often judged on what they wear or how their hair is." Over the year, his co-host Lisa Williamson's outfits were commented upon and criticized regularly. His unusual experiment proved just how much of a double standard there is.[21]

The gender gap has widened in the media arena with vast consequences. Women have been conditioned to emulate and seek this self-sabotaging attention. Let me share an example of the type of negative precedent this can set in the business world.

Erika, a senior partner at a large law firm in New York City, writes, "The dressing for success, for business women needs updating . . . Male partners are coming to me to ask how they address younger associates who are showing cleavage or wearing dresses or skirts that are too short as they sit around the

---

21 From www.CBS News.com, November 17, 2014.

board room table in the midst of billion dollar negotiations. Some of the senior partners won't staff big deals with these women, who may be very talented, simply because of their outfits. They fear the harassment allegations, and they don't want such women to taint the integrity of their law firm."

Nobody was going to go knocking on the young lawyers' doors to tell them the way they were dressing for work was inappropriate. The hard work those smart women put into getting into law school, not to mention the grueling bar exam itself, was unfairly and unnecessarily undermined simply because they believed their business attire didn't matter. No one taught them this. It went unspoken.

.....

"The woman should be the message; not the clothes."

—NINA MCLEMORE

When you get dressed, it pays to be conscious of what you are trying to achieve and what motivations may be contributing to your choices. Are you attempting to look like a magazine model because that's what you have been pressured to do? Given what we are discussing here, take a moment to consider what image you want to portray and whether or not your current (and perhaps unconscious) choices are drawing negative attention or opportunity.

Dealing with the Opposite Sex

As we discussed in our previous chapters, workplace diversity is key to superior outcomes. Businesswomen and businessmen complement and challenge one another on our different mindsets and competencies. But we have to face the facts: Working with men also presents us with challenges we need to be aware of and prepared for. While businessmen have the best of intentions and display professional behavior at work, studies show that *men in general still think about sex an average of nineteen times a day.*[22] These are your coworkers, your clients, and your bosses. If you choose to dress in a blouse that reveals cleavage or a skirt that leaves nothing to the imagination, you've created an unwanted distraction of someone you're trying to have an important discussion with.

Whether he's looking at your chest or legs or trying not to, he's not likely going to be listening to what you have to say if you're showing too much skin. You might as well pack up and go home because you probably won't accomplish what you want to. Why put yourself in that position? Don't! Sexy won't get you ahead for long, but being smart and professional will.

By dressing well, we have the power to reverse the negative stereotypes. It won't happen overnight. We're in this for the long haul, and the more of us out there who are willing to make an effort to shut this negative attention down, not even

---

22 Tom Stafford, "How Often Do Men Really Think about Sex?," *BBC*, June 18, 2004, http://www.bbc.com/future/story/20140617-how-often-do-men-think-about-sex.

giving it the opportunity to arise, the quicker the business world will start to shift in our favor.

The Bottom Line

We hear the message over and over: "It's what's on the inside that counts." And that's true. You will absolutely not advance in your career if your ABCs aren't strong, if you're unable to prioritize your values and work toward them, or if you're unable to show others what's on the inside through critical communication skills. In an ideal world, this would be enough to lead us to the top. In an ideal world, appearances wouldn't matter. Unfortunately, that's not the world we live in. Maybe this will change in the next decades—we can certainly hope so—but right now, I am here to tell you that in the business world, people still judge the book by its cover. Hopefully, this chapter has changed the minds of skeptics who think otherwise by proving that dressing well isn't simply a matter of acquiescing to that truth: Dressing the part can help us work harder, get over our Imposter Syndrome, and start to fight negative stereotypes.

Generations of women have fought heroically to fortify our rights to be treated equally in society and in the workplace. Be the example for the next generation in how we comport ourselves by dressing to support our goals as individuals and unified women. The way to move forward is to be aware of how differently we think, stop self-sabotaging, and leave the worn-out, limiting beliefs of negative attention behind. And we need to bring other women along with us.

Monitoring and improving your professional image are not optional if you're serious about your career. What you look like on the outside is the ticket that gets you through the door. It causes people to sit up and take notice and to listen to what you have to say. It encourages people to take you and what you bring to the table seriously. Once you understand the unspoken rules of dressing for success, you will transform yourself and ignite your career.

What Is No One Telling You?

THINGS TO REMEMBER . . .

- We are always being judged by how we look, how we carry ourselves, and what comes out of our mouths. When you're judging others, others are judging you, too. It's just the way it is.

- If the first impression is made poorly, it's difficult to change. Make it count.

- Stop the negative attention cycle the media denotes. Get the right attention for the right reasons—your brains and your professional image.

- The more professional you present yourself, the more professional the work outflow will be.

PLAN OF ACTION

As a result of what I learned in chapter 7, I am going to

Stop doing—

- _____

- _____

Start doing—

- _____

- _____

Continue doing—

- _____

- _____

Chapter Eight

how to dress the part: creating the right image to make a lasting impression

.....

*"If you don't have time to do it right, when
will you have time to do it over?"*

–JOHN WOODEN

An executive came into our office one morning to speak at our meeting. He was late, and when he finally arrived, his top button was undone and his tie was askew. I nudged my partner and said, "Jason, look how disheveled he looks." "Yeah, he really does," Jason agreed. The man's first impression didn't make the grade, and his image took our attention away from his presentation. His appearance didn't inspire confidence, and he lost the chance for us to want to introduce him to our clients. He didn't project the image of success that would align with that of our group.

Deborah Reynolds from Face Image Consulting, Inc., writes, "It's important to create a good first impression, but essential to create a lasting impression." How can you cement that positive first impression you've worked so hard to create? It takes effort and planning. What lasting impression are *you* leaving?

Now that we've covered the *whys* of dressing well, let's talk about the *hows*. Unlike our male counterpart (outside of looking disheveled like the speaker above), who simply pairs his suit with a shirt, tie, and appropriate colored shoes, women's wear is trickier. We have many more choices to make when putting an outfit together. This chapter will help you navigate those choices by giving you the tips and tools you need to make dressing the part as straightforward and streamlined as possible. Women are more scrutinized than men, and with the number of choices out there on what to wear and how to wear it, making a mistake can hurt our professional image unnecessarily. Like I said in the last chapter, it's not fair, but it's the reality, and in order to change the work culture of the future, we must first learn how to navigate its current unspoken rules.

Here's what you need to know: Your wardrobe positions you either in or out of the advancement pool. And yet, nobody is willing to tell us this truth or explain how we can address it with success! Your friends don't want to hurt your feelings, your boss may fear an uncomfortable discussion that could lead to an HR issue, your colleagues don't want to risk tension in the workplace, and prospective clients will simply choose not to work with you. So this message goes unspoken. But you deserve to know what it takes to make sure you're "in" that pool. We all know what "business professional" looks like, but it seems too many of us are afraid of making these rules clear. Consider this chapter your ultimate "how to." It is comprised of the tips and tricks of style I've learned during my three decades in business.

COMMON EXCUSES FOR NOT PAYING ATTENTION TO OUR APPEARANCE

As we discussed at length in chapter two, women lead busy lives. Considering all of the responsibilities on our plates, it would be easy to stop prioritizing our appearance. Sometimes, the extra half hour it takes to do your hair and makeup feels like an unworthy use of your time, especially if it's cutting into time with kids or with a spouse or with other priorities. But those extra minutes are an investment in your professional future. Take my word for it: Regardless of what you're juggling at home, coming to the office disheveled is not an option. Sure, it's more work. But if you're serious and want to succeed in the business world, you have to make sure you can meet and even exceed appearance expectations. So let's take a look at some common excuses women give, and break them down one by one:

- **I don't understand why it's a big deal.** It is a big deal if you're spinning your wheels when you don't fit the part. That's called self-sabotage.

Continued

- **I'm too busy.** This is an excuse for being lackadaisical with one's appearance.
- **I should be able to express who I am and be myself.** No, that is not true during business hours. It's a uniform. End of story.
- **My style has been working for me for years.** It's easy to become set in our ways while life moves forward and styles change, along with the definition of business professional.
- **I don't know how.** Some of us have never been taught how to dress professionally, but that doesn't mean we don't owe it to ourselves to try.

Tip 1: Dress with Thought!

Close your eyes for a moment. Imagine you're getting ready in the morning, knowing that you have an important appointment you've been working on for over a year. In your mind, go into your closet and think about what you're going to wear— your best selection. Now, make that outfit your new bar for what you're going to wear to work every day, because you never know when a business prospect will present itself.

- Wear clothing that fits properly. Your skirt or pants should pass the swish test, meaning they aren't so tight you can't shift them around on your hips.

- Your blouse shouldn't gap or pull open across your

chest. Keep double-sided tape at your office in case the blouse "shrinks."

- Skirts or dresses shouldn't be higher than a horizontal finger-width or two above the knee. Make sure your skirt doesn't ride up your thigh when you sit down or kneel.

- Keep heels three inches high or under (most professional height is under three inches) to work. Shoes should be business-appropriate—not casual.

- Don't wear a sleeveless top or dress in a professional setting. If your blouse is sleeveless, keep a jacket on. Clothes should be comparable to a man's suit. You wouldn't expect to see a man in a sleeveless tank, unbuttoned shirt, no socks, or inappropriate shoes. Follow that lead. If the temperatures are soaring and perspiring is a big issue, still take a light cotton or linen jacket with you and wear the jacket for the shortest time possible. Note: Why do you think men wear undershirts with their button-down shirts? To absorb the perspiration. They add, not subtract. Check.

- Be a minimalist when it comes to jewelry. You do not want to distract from what you're saying. Pearls are still a uniform staple when you're dealing with the wide range of age groups we encounter at the office.

- Skip the sheer clothing, even with a slip or a camisole. Sheer shrugs are not office attire either.

- Skip the perfume and heavy makeup.

Tip 2: You Never Know Who You'll Run Into Outside of the Office

Classy dress is essential—this is true for outside the office as well. If your work is so close to home that you'll bump into clients, be cognizant of what you wear in social situations. If you run into a client and their friend during a weekend dinner, for example, you could miss an opportunity for a referral if you're not looking the part. Here's an example:

While house hunting in Florida, Jerry and I were interested in a particular area, so we inquired with the locals we met if they liked living there: people at the grocery store, the bank—everywhere. In a restaurant, a couple and a woman who looked like their daughter who had just finished lunch sat next to us. We asked if they liked the area, and we shared that we were exploring the housing market.

"Well, we actually just closed on our house today. We've lived in the area for years and we just bought another house," the wife said. "This is our real estate agent." She gestured to the woman with them.

The agent jumped at the opportunity and asked us if we'd like to look at houses the following day. She was dressed professionally, which gave us the impression that she knew what she was doing. We agreed. The next day, we met her and looked at houses. We ended up buying the first house she showed us. What a successful day that turned out to be for her, and it happened because she was dressed to make a great first impression.

·····

"I believe luck is preparation meeting opportunity. If
you hadn't been prepared when the opportunity came
along, you wouldn't have been lucky."

−OPRAH WINFREY

Tip 3: Overdress to Impress

Our business has a number of professional athletes as clients, and when they come into town we get together. Although the location is usually in a casual setting, they are clients, so I wouldn't show up in a tee shirt and jeans, even if that's what most others are wearing. I choose something like pants with a blazer, a white cotton shirt, and pearls. It's better to be a bit overdressed than underdressed. Business is business. Even if it's a casual affair, you are there on a serious matter, whatever profession you are in. Standing out in a positive way won't happen if you are blending in, wearing a tee shirt and jeans. You don't need to match the informality of your environment. Be pulled together by distinguishing yourself as the professional they hired or want to hire. Know your audience, environment, and culture. Match it. Then step it up a notch.

Casual Friday is another important way you can set yourself apart and use your clothing as a way of indicating you're serious about your career. Before dressing down on casual Friday, ask yourself this: "If my best client shows up today, will I be underdressed?" The more casual the garment, the higher caliber of clothing is required. Think J. Crew or Ann Taylor as a good go-to for conservative designer apparel.

Some years back, I dressed down on a Friday, a day there were no in-office appointments. Wouldn't you know, a celebrity client popped into the office unannounced. Knowing my casual appearance didn't make the right impression affected my poise, and I wasn't on my A game. Dressing more professionally would have better met the client's expectations. Undoubtedly, it also would have given me the confidence to handle his surprise visit.

I ran into an acquaintance of mine at a charity fund-raising event. Jackie whispered to me that she'd invited a client and his wife whom she hadn't met yet to join her because she was hoping to get more business from them. Jackie was wearing a short dress and very high heels. The client and his wife were dressed more conservatively. The client's wife gave Jackie the once-over with a disapproving glare. She watched Jackie talk to her husband and wasn't impressed.

Even when your professionalism is exemplary, dealing with the opposite sex can be tricky, especially when spouses are involved. Beware and take care. When in doubt, make it the conservative option. If the spouse or significant other of a client or prospective client doesn't feel 110 percent comfortable with your appearance and manner at work or any other place they see you, it's going to be game over.

If in doubt about an outfit's appropriateness, give it a "dress rehearsal" before an important meeting or function. When you're wearing your outfit for the "dress rehearsal" and you are getting a stare from someone, man or woman, at a specific body part from what seemed right but really is too tight, too low, too short, too revealing of a garment, take note. If you get a second stare, you will know that it's not appropriate for your meeting or function. It goes unspoken but needs to be addressed.

Tip 4: Look Current

When someone looks at you, they believe what they see is what they'll get. You project your company's image and reputation. Clients won't risk being embarrassed by recommending someone who shows up to a meeting looking unprofessional. You can be brilliant at what you do, but if you're sloppy, wearing suggestive clothing, or look outdated, your clients will perceive everything you say as sloppy, not serious, and outdated.

If you are cutting edge in business, reinforce this in your appearance by looking chic and current. When you look classy and sharp, it shows you care enough to be your best, and that flows over into everything you do. Don't let your choices limit you. This includes updating hairstyles and eyewear, two important areas in the three-second-impression arena. Keep hair polished if longer and chic if shorter. Don't be afraid to go bold with your eyeglasses, and steer clear of bifocal lines or readers whenever possible. Remember that while you're always marketing yourself, it's imperative to have an edge. Staying current plays a big role in this.

Tip 5: Dress for Geographical Region and Culture

I've mentioned how much more difficult the choice of what to wear is for women than men, but clothing does give women a distinct advantage: We have the unique opportunity to immediately and nonverbally convey a certain level of thoughtfulness and awareness to clients. This is especially true when interacting with clients from different cultures. When you're dressing for your client, considering their background can make a big impact. For example, in certain parts of the world, some colors are not acceptable. You won't typically see a Chinese person wearing white because it symbolizes mourning for them. Some cultures say the back of your neck or your toes shouldn't be exposed. People in New York dress differently than people in Los Angeles. And people in Helsinki dress differently than people in Shanghai. Although your clothing choices should represent you, consider the geographical region and culture of people and places you visit, and dress accordingly. Whenever you're traveling out of your region or have international guests in town, research professional dress norms of the culture through a human resources connection of the company you'll be on business with, for example, or ask a local contact.

Tip 6: Shop Less, Dress Better

What if all of the clothes in your closet fit perfectly and looked good? Then, making the right choices wouldn't be a big deal in the morning when you're rushed for time. The problem is that when we look in our closet full of options and can't seem to put an outfit together, our *impulse is to buy more.* When we get to the store, we buy pieces that appeal to us and often don't consider how that garment will work with our existing wardrobe. Then, even after shopping, we still don't have anything to wear.

Buying garments randomly won't necessarily enlarge or improve your wardrobe. The truth is, if you look at your closet, you're probably only wearing about 20 to 30 percent of the clothes you own. The other 80 percent of clothing in your closet doesn't fit right, doesn't complement your shape, or isn't practical for some other reason. Eventually, these garments become outdated, without ever being worn much. Sound familiar? Shopping without a strategy means that most of what you buy will probably end up in the unworn 80 percent of your closet. Instead, challenge yourself to *shop with intention.*

Shopping with intention is going into the store with an objective and choosing your clothing and accessories accordingly.

Anytime you need to shop for new clothes, bring a list of the things you're looking for. Doing so helps prevent costly impulse purchases and ensures you won't be faced with a full closet and nothing to wear. Update your list when you realize you need a certain item, such as a particular colored belt. If you don't add it to the list immediately, you'll likely forget it. Shopping with a list and with intention will allow you to think objectively about how a certain piece will go with what you currently own.

When you're looking at clothes in a store, keep in mind what complements your body type and what looks best on you. For example, if you like shirt collars because you can flip the collar up—a look which elongates your neck—focus on those styles in the store. If you're fond of a certain style blouse and it complements you, buy more of them. If you find shoes that are comfortable and look professional, buy two colors—especially if they're on sale. Don't be afraid of color. Buy what makes you feel confident and you look good in.

Your closet should only hold top-notch power clothes that maintain your A-game appearance. You'll look sharp while stretching your dollar by interweaving your existing favorites with current styles rather than purchasing or pairing random garments without a plan. Making strategic wardrobe decisions before you step into the store will save time and money and will make shopping so much easier. It will also give you more cash to invest in your 401(k).

CREATE A STYLE FOLDER–SHOP YOUR OWN CLOSET

I keep a manila folder of professional looks I like that I've seen in magazines and online catalogs. Begin yours by reviewing a few magazines and online catalogs. Find something that catches your eye? Start with eliminating what sells an idea–the attractive model–by covering her face and hair and envisioning yours there instead. Still like it? Then tear out or print the photos of the looks that appeal to you. Another option would be to create a style board on Pinterest. You'll have professionally styled looks at your fingertips from which you can take pieces from your closet. Mix, match, and improvise. The goal is to gather styles that you wouldn't put together on your own. Go through the folder once every other year to eliminate anything that's outdated. It only takes a few minutes. Creating and maintaining this style folder will expand your wardrobe possibilities without the need to add a lot of new clothes to your closet. When you have an important meeting or presentation to prepare for, take out your folder and, at a glance, you'll get multiple A-game ideas.

Tip 7: Find a Style Avatar

Observe the unspoken dress codes in your work environment. Pay attention to how people in different positions dress, taking particular note of women executives in positions to which you aspire. Make them your style avatar. Take note of what they're wearing and how they're wearing it. However, be cautious about modeling a woman who has been in the business for twenty-plus years and has earned a professional reputation, allowing her more wardrobe freedom. A friend of mine—a successful corporate attorney, Beth Gotthelf, who has worked to achieve professional prominence—dresses like a hip bohemian even for a day in the courtroom. I wondered how she got away with this, so I asked her if she had always dressed that way. "Are you kidding me?" she said. "I had those shirts and flappy bow ties in the late eighties we had to wear. Oh, you better believe it." Beth was successful for a number of years before she earned the leeway to create her own image because her reputation preceded her. Take that into account when observing and emulating successful women; their rules may not apply to you yet.

Don't be afraid to ask a woman from your office for help. She'll likely be flattered. Ask her where she shops. Take notes on how she puts her outfits together. Seek, observe, and emulate what you know to be true, and be real about what's not.

Tip 8: Personal Grooming— Be Thoughtful

Personal grooming is as fundamental to professional appearance as clothing. Just as professional appearance can speak volumes about who we are and what we stand for without us uttering a single word, personal grooming can make us stand out for the wrong reasons. Being considerate of the people around us is paramount, so keep personal hygiene habits that will allow people to engage with you without being distracted by all-too-personal problems. Following is a list of personal grooming tips I've found to be particularly helpful:

- *Too much cologne and perfume.* This doesn't work! If you must wear it, it should be so subtle that only a significant other can smell it when close to you. There's nothing worse than perfume so overbearing that it makes someone ill or sets off their allergies. Instead of engaging with you, they'll just want to get you out the door.

- *Bad breath.* Make sure to keep up with your oral hygiene by flossing daily and scheduling dental cleanings regularly. Avoid garlic or onions at lunch if you have clients in the afternoon. Who wants to be remembered as the person with the foul breath?

- *No chewing gum at work.* It takes away from your professionalism, especially when you nervously chomp on it, and distracts coworkers.

- *Hair.* Keep it neat and fresh looking. If it's shorter, make the look chic. If it's longer, keep it trimmed. If you tend to play with your hair, keep it in a ponytail so you don't. Playing with hair makes you look immature and takes away your credibility. Keep your roots freshly touched up. There are hair powders you can buy from the drugstore that will cover your roots until you can make it to the salon.

- *Nails.* Keep them manicured and polished with a neutral color. If you do use color, then keep nails short.

- *Shoes.* Keep shoes polished with a polish sponge. Monitor your heels to make sure they remain scuff free and heel tips remain like new.

- *Makeup.* Makeup is expected. Keep it neutral. The idea is to wear makeup without looking like you're wearing much makeup at all. Too much makes you look cheap, and no makeup makes you look tired.

- *Accessories.* Be a minimalist. Earrings should not dangle more than an inch. No bangles. Funky necklaces work if they are in good taste.

- *Properly ironed clothes.* There is nothing less impressive than walking into a morning meeting with badly wrinkled clothing. It didn't get that wrinkled on your way in, unless you're wearing linen—stay away from linen!

- *Handbags.* Keep these quality, streamlined, and in good condition. Don't overstuff a bag; It makes you look disorganized—and no large logos, please.

- Do a "background check" via a mirror looking at your behind before you leave the house. The clothes should lie smoothly to avoid panty lines. If it can't be solved, consider a blazer. It also solves running out the door with a dress bottom tucked into pantyhose (I bought a mirror for the women's restroom at the office to not have that happen again!) or a large run in the back of the leg of your winter tights.

Tip 9: Your Style Extends Beyond Your Clothes

Your clothes may be the most immediate, tangible reflection of your image, but the spaces and objects people associate with you need to be monitored as well. The cleanliness of your surroundings reflects you and your professionalism. Thus, your office should be clean and uncluttered. Likewise, your car should be immaculate inside and out, especially if you meet or drive clients. Inspire confidence in all your dealings.

A NOTE ON BUSINESS CARDS

Unless you are an entrepreneur, you may not have much say in what your business card looks like. But to the degree possible, have them stand out. Keep the standard size, but consider using an upscale paper stock—something with a suede feel, for example. When you give it to people, they'll notice how it feels and remember you were the one with the unique card. Leave the back of your card blank so people

Continued

can jot down a note describing where they met you or why they wanted to contact you.

When someone gives you his or her business card, treat it as a gift. The average person, when given a business card, often doesn't even look at it before tucking it into a pocket or in their purse. In Japan, the custom is to look at the business card, read it in front of the person who handed it to you, and say thank you. It shows appreciation for the other person sharing his or her knowledge and respect, and the person who gives you his or her card will remember that. Moreover, if you want to write on the back of someone's card, ask permission first. Don't treat it like a piece of scrap paper. This makes the card itself and the act of exchanging cards an honoring experience.

Make a promise to yourself to write down where you met the contact and any intention of a future connection. How many business cards have you found in your wallet or pocket a month later that you toss out because you can't remember the details? A good rule of thumb: Connect within twenty-four hours. If you don't value the connection with urgency, they won't value a response with urgency—energy begets energy.

Tip 10: Seek Professional Help

Hiring a stylist may seem extravagant, but the benefits of making this investment can far outweigh the cost. Anyone in the spotlight knows the importance and value of having a stylist.

It's no different for you. You are in the spotlight as a business-woman in a male-dominated business world. Hire a stylist at least once to get the drift of what a difference they make in your image. My stylist, Jon Lieckfelt, has never steered me wrong in perfect A-game apparel for important speaking engagements. I've always had compliments on whatever he's purchased for me, and he always has found a bargain for me.

A stylist's services may cost anywhere from $2,500 to $5,000, including clothes. Consider it an investment in your future. You have a $100,000 education. Invest a few thousand dollars in your walking business card. A stylist will prevent you from making choices that don't work for you, which cost time and money—like the clothes that end up unworn and in the back of your closet. If your budget is tight, you can't afford clothes you won't wear long term. It's better to have ten or twelve A-game quality outfits than twenty run-of-the-mill looks.

Make sure that whatever personal stylist you hire has cor-porate image and training experience. Some stylists think they can put everyone in shorter skirts and four-inch heels, wasting their time and your money if they can't help you enhance your appearance in the business environment. Be open to what they bring you, but also communicate your goal ahead of their shopping excursion. Not everything the stylist brings you will fit your personal style. Tell the stylist what you won't wear, whether that's a dress, three-fourth-length sleeves, or wide legs. The stylist should take notes of your business culture and client base. They should provide references, be willing to shop at all levels of retailers, be clear on how they get paid, and understand your day (time on feet, travel, your movement in presentations, etc.). You two are a team, but you're the boss. If something doesn't sit with you, be up front with your stylist.

HOW A STYLIST CAN HELP YOU BREAK FREE OF THE IMPOSTER SYNDROME

Hiring a stylist can be an important step toward breaking the Imposter Syndrome, as mentioned in the previous chapter. Beth Morrison, president of a large nonprofit organization serving victims of domestic violence and sexual abuse, shares her story:

"As far back as I can recall, I have had body image issues. When I became the CEO of a high-profile nonprofit, those nagging concerns crept to the forefront of my thinking. I had fears that I would not be taken seriously by community leaders, donors, and others because of my body shape and appearance. I didn't feel that I fit the mold of an executive. I know that these fears and the lack of confidence that went along with them did in fact hold me back. I was rather successful at what seemed like faking it, but I knew that faking it would only get me so far.

"As I approached my forty-fifth birthday, a colleague of mine encouraged me to enter a contest for a free professional makeover. This colleague knew me well enough to know that I didn't have much self-confidence in my appearance and in my role as a nonprofit leader. Makeup, hair, clothing, and accessories don't mean very much to me. To this day, I would much rather be found in shorts and a tee shirt instead of a suit and heels.

"As luck would have it, the woman who never wins a thing won the contest for the makeover. And with huge, I mean *huge*, reservations and a bit of an attitude, I accepted this gift. What a gift it was!

"With the guidance of a consultant, I discovered that I did have style (who knew!), and she taught me some basic simple techniques, which turned my disdain for shopping into something I can now enjoy. My comfort level grew in knowing what clothes work and don't work, and my confidence in my leadership abilities also grew. Over time, I no longer believed that I didn't belong at the table."

.....

"You can be considered unattractive in our culture and have great style. You can have no money and have great style. You can have a lot of money and great style—more often you'll have terrible style. You plaster yourself in what you think you should be wearing and you've lost yourself."

−TOM FORD

Nailing It—Every Time

A woman's success wardrobe is current and classy. It transcends age and culture smoothly and timelessly. You'll make a fresh, attractive impression on clients, colleagues, and contacts. Most important, a solid success wardrobe is as unique as the woman who wears it.

Dressing for success isn't lackluster. On the contrary, you can have style and flare and still be businesslike by having the right arsenal at your fingertips. Mix your personal style with current fashion trends, making it your own unique image. Not everyone is gifted with a knack for fashion, but expert help is at your fingertips when you use these strategies.

What Is No One Telling You?

THINGS TO REMEMBER . . .

- You are your walking business card, in the office and out of the office as well. If you might bump into clients after hours, keep that in mind. Look clean and neat at the grocery store. Be tasteful in your date night apparel. It's classier anyway.

- Think classy and modern, current and professional, and update your hair, makeup, eyewear, and clothing every few years. It gives the impression that you are on top of your game and are cutting edge.

- Remember, you are dealing with people of all different ages in the workplace. You should appeal to all of them.

- Do you feel good in what you're wearing?

- Is this the image you want to portray?

- Don't buy anything without looking at your backside in the mirror. Bring a small handheld mirror in your purse or snap a selfie.

- Make your tailor your BFF. Your tailor can make an "off the rack" outfit look like a designer piece with the right nips and tucks.

- Wait until you have obtained success to dress "outside the box." It's the success allowing the freedom to dress, not loosely dressed to bequest success.

PLAN OF ACTION

As a result of what I learned in chapter 8, I am going to

Stop doing–

- _____

- _____

Start doing–

- _____

- _____

Continue doing—

- _____

- _____

Conclusion

.....

"What would you do if you weren't afraid?"

–SPENCER JOHNSON

N o matter where you are or what you're up against, you can succeed in achieving your career goals. As the saying goes, *Shoot for the moon and land among the stars.* In an office filled with ninety-five men, I made it from being an entry-level woman employee with a child in tow to a top advisor. No one handed me the opportunities. I made opportunities, and you can too.

The code has gone unspoken for long enough. You now have the tools to handle any situation you come across with strength and perseverance. Remember your sisu!

We owe a lot to the women who came before us and paved the way. Let's not forget that, at one time, we couldn't vote or hold an executive career, not to mention the countless other rights that weren't available to women. We've come a long way, but it's still not far enough. In the past twenty years, we've balanced out and even surpassed men in education and ambitions. Yet not enough has changed—men still hold most of the top positions and many women are still not compensated as well as men are for the same work.

Ladies, our sisters, friends, daughters, and nieces are watching us closely. Are high aspirations worth the effort? You know it! We must push ourselves in what can sometimes be an inhospitable business environment. No longer do we sit back, feeling excluded or disrespected. We hike to the top of the mountain and out of the valley of disenchantment.

We spoke about the Unspoken Code in three parts. First, set yourself up for success so you exude confidence and honor yourself. This comes from within, even if you don't feel fully confident yet. It will come! Reach out to mentors, friends, and women's networking groups who get it and are ready to support you. Use them to be the wind beneath your wings.

Second, be an office power player by having the right communication tools. You'll close this book knowing how to position yourself for validation, respect, and ultimately, great success. You are stronger than you think. Keep believing in yourself and projecting confidence to the world. What you think of yourself is what you become.

And last, dress the part. Staying on your A game every day keeps you prepared for any opportunity that comes your way. If you want to stand out professionally, there's no second chance when it comes to the first impression. Remember the story of the real estate agent whose new client she met at a restaurant bought the first house she showed them the next day? It happens. Your next opportunity could walk up to you tomorrow. How will you be dressed to invite this professional opportunity?

Changing the way you think and communicate along with making a concerted effort on how you dress may feel like hard work at first, making the climb to success look steeper. Keep the endgame in mind. In the next five years, you can either make headway toward achieving your dreams or not. The choice is yours.

The road ahead may not be the easiest one at first. Nothing worthwhile is. The Unspoken Codes have been shared. What will enter your life that you don't even know about or haven't created a space for yet?

Keep this book as a reference to use for exercises and strategies when you need to remind yourself about what to do when old habits arise.

Join an executive network of women in your community (or use the sources listed in this book) to keep your momentum going. Before long, the Unspoken Code will feel like second nature to you and you'll be mentoring the new kids on the block. Each ledge you land on will prepare you to climb the next ledge you need to reach for the top. The view is incredible. We're waiting for you.

.....

"There is no tool for development more effective than the empowerment of women."

–KOFI ANNAN

Acknowledgments

My unconventional upbringing brought me into adult life earlier than most, but I realize that without those sometimes-challenging life experiences, I wouldn't be the person I am today. Looking back, I am thankful for my mother, whose passed on her impeccable fashion sense from her modeling days, and for my dad, who set high standards and encouraged me to enter the world of finance.

They say it takes a village to accomplish significant things . . . In my case, it took a city. It started on a lifetime family trip to Italy. Enjoying an after-dinner limoncello at a quaint outdoor café, my adult children, Larry and Kristen, encouraged me to take the first step to follow my passion of so long. The first step is the biggest one. Thanks, you two!

My husband and business partner, Jerry, supported me during the four years it took to get this book written. In the interim, our life took a major turn as we received news of Jerry's diagnosis of multiple myeloma cancer. Going through a stem cell transplant, we made it as positive of an experience one possibly can, looking for the silver lining as each day unfolded. Thank you, Jerry, for your can-do attitude, patience, and vulnerability as we continue our journey. I continue to pray for you.

Thanks also to our incredible staff at work—Jason, Peter, Mike, Kristen, and Sara—along with the most supportive clients and a good bull market. Thank you, gang.

To my personal assistant, Renea Callery, who willfully took calls, texts, and emails during nights and weekends and has a heart as big as the ocean.

To my artist siblings, Jo-Jo and Johnny, who I leaned on when deciding on the color combos for the book and website designs.

To my friends and other family, who I reached out to many times for their opinions for the book. In particular, Marie Remboulis, Karen Beisch, Tiina Paris, Pierre Corriveau, Dr. Paula Kilgore, Sandy Stilwell, Branka and Dan Megler, Beth Morrison, Kat Segovia, Julie Megler, St. Charles Bookies, Eeva Perttu, Alan, Rachelle Nozero, Alicia Masse, Harriet Shakir, Pat Wiggenhorn, Vanessa, David Ratner, Cathy Lewis, Eunice Gould, Linda Orlans, Ellen and Larry Miller, and Gary McLouth.

To my mentors, Paul Camilleri and Clarence Catallo, who believed in me from the beginning and were with me on my journey longer than just about anyone outside of my family.

To Greenleaf Book Group, who made this all possible.

Thank you, Justin, Tyler, Kat, Lindsey, Karina, Stevie, Stephanie, Kim, and Tanya, for your patience and perseverance in working with this first-time author.

Lastly, I thank all those not mentioned but were a part of my journey. You've all been the wind beneath my wings.

Index

About the Author

Marja Norris is the CEO and founder of MarjaNorris.com, a company dedicated to helping women achieve their career goals with style and confidence. With a distinguished career in finance, Marja has successfully navigated the male-dominated business world and is passionate about coaching women on how to be taken seriously, be heard, and get what they want at work.

A Top 100 Barron's Woman Advisor and graduate of the Parsons New School in Manhattan in summer intense fashion design, Marja has studied under the finest fashion designer professors in the world and was a contributing author to the book *Hot Mama in (High) Heels*. Marja's mission is to provide women with the tools to awaken the dreams in their hearts and help them blossom into everything they can be.

Marja is an alumnus of the board of directors for Haven for victims of domestic violence and is a supporter of the Multiple Myeloma Research Foundation. A portion of all profits from book proceeds are donated to Haven and MMRF. She lives in Michigan with husband Jerry and is a mother to two adult children.

2017
10/18: 6x read 9/18